HERE'S MY STORY

G&LR BOOKS
www.glreview.org

Library of Congress Cataloguing-in-Publication Data

Allison Armijo, editor
Here's My Story: Personal Essays from *The G&LR*

ISBN 979-8-9888150-3-7

HERE'S MY STORY

Personal Essays
from
The Gay & Lesbian Review

EDITED BY ALLISON ARMIJO

G&LR BOOKS / BOSTON

Contents

Pivoting | 55

Wanting | 81

Protecting | 103

Celebrating | 129

Foreword

The inspiration for "Here's My Story" (HMS) as a feature on *The G&LR* website was the realization, some years ago, that we receive more personal histories and memoirs than anything else in our submissions box. As a general rule, we don't publish first-person pieces in the magazine, but clearly many readers were clamoring to tell the world about their experiences as LGBTQ people. So the demand was there, but it took a while for us to realize that *The G&LR* blog was an ideal outlet for such a forum of disparate voices from our community. The first stories began to appear in 2019, and hundreds have been published to date.

For the first few years, HMS was edited in-house and published sporadically. It was Allison Armijo who moved the column forward starting in early 2023. During their tenure as *The G&LR*'s web editor, Alli turned HMS into a popular weekly forum, curating the stories and proposals, selecting those that showed promise, and working with writers as needed to help them find their voice. The result has been a steady stream of fascinating personal vignettes in which writers talk about everything from their coming-out experiences and first loves to political involvements and spiritual journeys.

These stories are all available on our website (at GLReview.org). So why publish them as a book? Some of these accounts are just so good that we felt they deserve a second look and a new readership. In addition to selecting the "best of" the many stories we've run, Alli has organized them into a set of chapters that highlight common themes, such as "Pivoting" and "Protecting," providing a kind of dialog among the writers. That said, this is the kind of book that allows you to shop around, perhaps in search of a story that resonates with your own.

In addition to thanking Alli for shepherding this project forward, I'd like to thank the Leonard-Litz Foundation for an annual grant in support of its publication. The book's design and layout were carried out by Rick Fiala, who has, I think, done a wonderful job. Finally, let me thank *The G&LR* publisher (and my husband) Stephen Hemrick, who managed the overall production of the book that you see.

Here's My Story is meant to appeal to a wide readership, but our special hope is that these firsthand accounts of the LGBTQ experience will be read by those who may be in the early stages of exploring their gender or sexuality, or looking for voices that speak to their personal situation. Whoever you are, we hope you will enjoy these wonderful accounts from a wide spectrum of writers from around the U.S. and the world.

Richard Schneider Jr.
Editor-in-Chief, The G&LR

Introduction

As WEB EDITOR of *The Gay & Lesbian Review* for the past three years, I've had the immense privilege of working with people who write about what they were never taught to name in the first place. What it means to navigate the immigration system in the U.S., to experiment with gender identity in an online chatroom, to rekindle once-strained relationships with loved ones—these are their stories. Many of the authors explore the nuances of navigating colonial systems that use language as a vessel of control and belonging, safety and surveillance. There are authors whose stories are not able to be featured in this collection for fear of deportation, loss of employment, and other safety concerns.

The stories in this collection acknowledge the tension between language as a vessel for connection and expressions of alienation. Each of the six sections in this anthology is named broadly after actions we take to navigate the world: "Speaking," "Moving," "Pivoting," "Wanting," "Protecting," and "Celebrating."

The same systems that enable violence against lgbtq+ people disproportionately harm people of color, immigrants, and people with disabilities. We are privileged to celebrate these stories as a testament to queer strength and resilience, while also recognizing the irreconcilable violence that got us here. The luxury of sexual and gender identity exploration has its roots in the struggle against the exploitation and policing of Black and brown people. We are grateful for the multiplicity of their voices in the pages that follow.

To end on a personal note, not so long ago I wrote a fictional short story about a piece of wax having an existential crisis about melting, about changing shape and not being able to recognize itself. I was reconciling with my relationship to gender dysphoria, to grief and control: "Breaking down is not necessarily a loss, it helps you reshape what you have. That's what wax does," the red wax says to the blue. This story is one of the most personal things I've ever written. Language rescued what my body could not, gave me space to explore the terror and hope of becoming, of finding myself in names and places I never had the courage to look for.

Allison Armijo
Web Editor, The G&LR

Speaking

A Jehovah's Witness is outed as gay and, standing in a motel shower, has a revelation about himself. A Filipino-American museum professional comes out to his Catholic family. A Jewish boy's hidden desires are awakened by the art he sees in his synagogue. The following stories explore the negotiation between rules spoken and unspoken, the language we use to reinscribe ourselves and others in the world around us.

My Journey to Asylum in America

By Edafe Okporo

HERE IS THE STORY of my journey to America as a gay asylum seeker.

It was my birthday in 2016. Early in the morning night, I was startled awake by a loud noise. "Edafe! Edafe!" voices chanted from outside. "Open the door! We know you are gay, and we are going to kill you!" Members of a local hate group had gathered outside as a mob. The community where I lived in gathered and made me a target. I woke up with my heart pounding through my chest. I could not. I knew I needed to move quickly, but I was paralyzed. I thought I could run through the back window if they were at the front of my building. In just my underwear, I raced to the window, ready to jump. But my house had been surrounded by a mob of people.

Soon, they had broken down my door and dragged me into the streets. I was flogged with sticks, cutlasses, and anything else they could find, beating me unconscious while children sang and cheered and clapped behind us. *Gay! Gay! Gay!*

When I woke up in the clinic, I was confused. I worried I would not recover from the attack. I was told a good Samaritan had saved me, which was only a slight relief compared to the terrible pain I felt all over my body. *If there is a God, they just saved me,* I remember thinking. I wondered then if my family knew—about what happened to me, about why it happened.

Though there were so many mysteries about the attack, I knew one thing for certain: I wouldn't be alive much longer if I stayed in Nigeria.

I fled to the United Arab Emirates, but had to return to Nigeria because I could not seek asylum there as a gay person. Two months passed like a breeze. I was just pushing paper, making money to help pay Uche's rent, and minding my business and my safety. One day in October of 2016, I was in my office, digging through a pile of paperwork, when my phone buzzed. It was a text from Uche.

"Edafe, where are you?"

"I'm in the office," I replied.

"You have to leave now!" This message followed with a link to an article. Apparently, I was being given an award for my work as a grassroots advocate for the MSM (men who have sex with men) community. What should have been a proud moment quickly turned dark. Because of the Same Marriage Prohibition Act (SSMPA), community members were encouraged to alert local authorities to known homosexuals. And the article was already online. I could be turned in to the police, or killed.

This single blazing moment brought the end of my life in Nigeria. I had to run—the further, the better. I found myself running toward the highway, shouting and flailing my hands to hail a cab. When a cab finally stopped, the driver asked me where I was going. Though I was staying with Uche, I'd left my documents behind at my apartment. We sped towards my place. A strange sensation dawned on me: my time in my home country had come to an end.

Fearing someone would recognize me, I asked the driver to wait outside while I gathered my things. I drew a file from under my mattress containing all my certificates: diploma, birth certificate, the local government of origin card, and baptism certificate. I could only take enough clothing to fit into my backpack. I stood up to breathe and looked around. This was it. I found myself again leaving a place I had called home.

I had the cab take me to Uche's place a few miles away, where I could stay for a few days before anyone would suspect he was hiding me. None of my family knew where I was. I wanted to call them, especially my mother, to tell her I was leaving with no plans to return. But I couldn't risk my safety—or theirs. If I succeed in escaping, my mother would be able to speak to me one day. I wasn't ready to give my life for my freedom. I wanted both. The real challenge lay on the other side of the Atlantic.

"What brings you to America?" the airport security guard asked me. He was a big, imposing man, with a clean-shaven head and a look on his face that betrayed nothing. Since I had a visitor's visa, I said I came for a two-week vacation. The officer looked at my passport, looked up at me, and then stamped my passport. But then he lingered. He looked at me again and did not return my passport.

"Is everything okay?" I asked.

"You just need to undergo further inspection." He stepped out of the box. "This way, sir, please follow me," he said kindly.

From the airport, I was taken to a detention center. The process of seeking asylum is always complex, but I was utterly alone in America. Worse, no one back home knew where I was, and I couldn't access my cellphone, which was taken from me before I entered the center. The calling cards from the center were very expensive, and I arrived in America with only $120. I worried about what my friends and family must have been thinking: Where was I? Was I safe? I thought especially of my mother, who was then living alone in Warri, hoping I would return from Abuja one day to come live nearby.

After five months and fourteen days, the day finally arrived. On April 18, 2017, an officer arrived to collect me. When I got into the court, the Judge asked; "What is your name and where are you from?" The questions progressed from easy answers—name and place of origin—to questions that took more thought. Why did I flee? Why wasn't I safe in Nigeria?

The goal was to convince the judge that I was in peril and would remain so unless I could stay in America. The stakes were high, but the time to deliberate was brief. The judge would have only two hours to decide my fate.

"Edafe Okporo, please rise," he said upon returning. "Thank you for your bravery and courage. I am granting you permission to live in America."

Around the world queer people face danger just for living their lives. Some of us make the hard decision to flee our homes in the hope of finding a new home. My journey is not unique in this respect. I tell it now because I know how important it is for LGBT people facing oppression to find home and an opportunity to rebuild their lives. ▫

Edafe Okporo is the executive director of Refuge America, a New York City-based nonprofit supporting LGBTQIA+ asylum seekers and refugees. As a former asylum seeker from Nigeria, he led New York's first shelter for asylum seekers and authored Asylum: A Memoir & Manifesto. *Edafe's work has been recognized by The David Prize, and he continues to build a country that welcomes everyone.*

The Unwritten Rules of Silence

*By Fendy Satria Tulodo**

IN THE DIM GLOW of a warung kopi (traditional coffee shop in Indonesia) in Surabaya, where the air is thick with cloves and fried tempeh, a conversation lingers over black coffee. Outside, motorbikes roar, vendors shout, dangdut (Indonesian folk music) blares from a passing angkot (share taxi). But here, in this pocket of stillness, Dimas sits across from Yusuf, his childhood friend, searching for words left unspoken for over a decade.

In Indonesia, some words carry the weight of culture, faith, and family honor. Some are never meant to be spoken at all.

Dimas had always known. Since the days the boys huddled over a single keyboard in an internet café, playing Counter-Strike, shoulders brushing. But Yusuf was different. He followed the rules. Prayed five times a day. Smiled when friends teased him about girls. He fit in effortlessly. Or so Dimas thought.

Then, in 2011, everything cracked open.

Dimas and Yusuf were walking home from school, taking the long way through damp alleys thick with the scent of grilled satay. Yusuf was quiet, his steps restless. Then, suddenly:

"I'm tired, Dim."

"Tired of what?"

Yusuf swallowed hard. "Have you ever felt like you wanted to be someone else?"

*The author's name has been changed to protect his privacy.

For Dimas, the words hit like a fist to the ribs.

Dimas forced a laugh. "We all want to be someone else. But we can't."

But that wasn't what Yusuf meant. And deep down, Dimas knew it.

That was the last day they spoke about it.

Years passed. Dimas moved to Jakarta for university, drowning in blueprints and late-night kopi tubruk (Indonesian-style coffee). Yusuf stayed in Surabaya, married a neighborhood girl, had two kids, ran a calligraphy business. From the outside, everything looked as it should. But in the quiet moments—between classes, in the back of a Gojek (ride-hailing service in Indonesia), staring at city lights—Dimas wondered about his friend.

Then, a text message out of nowhere: "Do you still remember me, Dim?"

And now, years later, here they are, sitting at a warung kopi once again. Older, but still abiding by the same silence. The same rules.

"You happy?" Dimas finally asks.

Yusuf stirs his coffee. "Have you ever heard about the man from my village who suddenly disappeared?"

Dimas frowns. "Who?"

Yusuf exhales, a hollow chuckle escaping. "The man who was caught being different."

The words hang heavy between them.

It's the kind of story that never makes the news but spreads in whispers— men disappearing, families vanishing out of shame. No laws are needed when the rules are written in glances, in unspoken warnings.

Dimas tightens his grip on his cup. "So?"

Yusuf looks up, something raw in his eyes. "I can't disappear, Dim. I have children."

And just like that, Dimas understands.

This isn't a confession. This isn't regret. This is just another unwritten rule.

Outside, the warung kopi hums with life. The scent of fried snacks mingles with exhaust fumes. Students laugh at the next table, a vendor calls out for bakso (Indonesian meatballs). Life moves forward, indifferent to the storm in the silence between them.

Dimas watches the dark liquid swirl in his cup. It tastes like regret, like all the words that were never spoken.

"So, what do you want?"

Yusuf exhales. "I don't know."

And maybe that's the most honest thing he's ever said.

For years, Dimas imagined this conversation differently. A desperate confession. A plea for help. A plan to escape. Something dramatic, something meaningful.

But instead, they are just two men, sipping coffee, trapped by their own realities.

Dimas lets out a bitter laugh. "I thought you reached out to talk. But you don't even know what you want."

Yusuf's jaw tightens. "I reached out because you're the only one who knows, Dim."

The only one who knows.

Dimas scans the warung (roadside stall)—men in peci (cap widely worn in Indonesia) discussing politics, a woman adjusting her hijab, an old vendor counting change. This city, this air, they all enforce the same law. Be normal. Be invisible. Do not disturb the balance.

"How does it feel?"

Yusuf smiles, but it never reaches his eyes. "Like standing at the edge of a cliff, every day."

Dimas looks down at his coffee, watching the ripples settle. There is nothing he can say to that.

Dimas wants to tell Yusuf that things are different now. That in Jakarta, he's met people who live freely, who have carved out spaces where they can exist without fear. But what good are those words here, in this warung, in this city where a single rumor can erase a man's existence?

"Have you ever tried to… leave?"

Yusuf's fingers tighten around his cup. "Leave what? My family? My children?"

Dimas stays quiet.

"You think I haven't thought about it?" Yusuf's voice is barely a whisper. "Every single day. But I'm not you."

Not you. The words sting. Dimas knows what he means. He is the one who got away. But it doesn't feel like freedom. Not when he's sitting here, listening to Yusuf's voice crack under the weight of his own reality.

For the first time, Yusuf has said it out loud. For the first time, the silence between them is broken.

Yusuf's confession lingers between them like burnt coffee—bitter, unshakable. The warung is still alive with conversation, but Dimas no longer hears it. His mind is fixed on the man across from him.

"So, what do you want me to say?"

Yusuf exhales sharply. "I don't know what to do, Dim."

Frustration swells in Dimas. He leans forward. "Which answer do you want, Yus? The one that sounds good, or the one that's true?"

Yusuf looks at him, and Dimas knows he understands. The truth is cruel. Yusuf already made his choice. He chose when he married, when he stayed, when he woke up each day and played his role. And yet…

"If I could redo everything… If I could go back to when we were in college…"

Dimas closes his eyes. He shouldn't ask, but he does anyway.

"Would you have chosen me?"

A long silence. Then, barely above a whisper: "Yes."

It's the answer Dimas has wanted for years. But now, it feels hollow.

Because "yes" doesn't change anything. "Yes" is just a ghost of a life they never had.

Dimas laughs bitterly. "Funny, isn't it?"

Yusuf shakes his head. "There's nothing funny about it."

Dimas wants to argue, but what's the point? They were once two boys who swore they'd never let the world change them. And yet, here they are—one pretending, the other still lost.

"Sometimes I see you in the news, on discussion panels," Yusuf says.

"And I think, that could have been me."

Dimas clenches his fists. "You can. You just don't want to pay the price."

Yusuf flinches. "Easy for you to say."

Dimas shakes his head. "No, Yus. It's not easy. I know the price. And I pay it every day."

The warung is quieter now, the air thick with everything they cannot say.

"So, what do you think I should do?"

Dimas stares at him for a long time. Then, softly, says: "Live."

The word hangs between them, heavier than anything else.

Because in the end, that's the only answer.

For a moment, Yusuf doesn't respond. The weight of the conversation settles deep in his bones. The warung feels emptier now. Someone outside lights a cigarette, the match flickering.

"Sometimes I feel like my life is just a waiting room," Yusuf murmurs.

Dimas frowns. "What do you mean?"

"Like I'm sitting somewhere, waiting for something that will never come."

Dimas exhales. "And now?"

Yusuf chuckles mirthlessly. "Now I realize, I'll never get that answer."

Dimas grips the table. He wants to say it's not too late.

But it is. They both know it.

"Sometimes I dream about you," Yusuf says suddenly. "We're back in the past. Riding a motorbike, eating meatballs by the street. Just talking about the future." He smiles, but it's tinged with sadness. "In those dreams… you're always there."

Dimas swallows. "Me too."

It's the closest they'll ever come to admitting what they've lost.

Yusuf leans back. "I should go home."

The words land heavy, final.

Dimas nods. "You've made your choice?"

A bitter smile. "I made my choice a long time ago, Dim."

They step outside, the city buzzing around them. Shadows stretch across the pavement, long and unspoken.

Yusuf lights a cigarette. Then, quietly, "If you ever need me, you know how to find me."

Dimas doesn't answer—just watches—as Yusuf walks away, disappearing into the night. Only when he's gone does Dimas pull out his phone. His fingers hover over the screen, over Yusuf's contact.

Then, after a moment, he locks the phone, shoves it back into his pocket, and walks in the opposite direction. Because some stories don't get a happy ending. Some stories just end.

From Malang, Indonesia, Fendy writes sharp stories about marginalized people. His writing explores hard choices when no one is perfect. Some are rebels looking for forgiveness, while others are powerful people who do bad things.

Coming Out Catholic, Without the Drama

By Justin Estoque

I GREW UP SCHOOLED IN Filipino Roman Catholic traditions by pious parents. In the late 1950s, when I was seven years old, Dad would dutifully drive the family to Mass at St. Joseph's Catholic Church every Sunday morning. Being the devout son that I was, it was not long before I became an altar boy.

Before Mass started, my altar boy partner and I would let ourselves into the sacristy and we'd pick out the crimson cassocks and white surplices, important and fabulous liturgical vestments. Once Mass started, we solemnly processed behind the priest entering the altar and genuflected with him as the parishioners came to their feet singing the hymn "Hail Holy Queen Enthroned Above." We carried bread and wine to the altar and shook the cluster of bells as the priest miraculously transformed the bread and wine into the body and blood of Christ. Being privy to holy, hidden church spaces for men only and allowed entry onto the sacred altar boosted my self-image. Not just any kid or adult had the privilege to partake in such rites. I also became a source of pride to my parents.

Later, as an out gay adult man, I could see how being an altar boy also offered the chance every week to don vestments that swished like a dress, and to cultivate close, secret friendships, perhaps bordering on the erotic, with other altar boys. But back then I could only imagine playing by the straight and narrow.

My altar boy experience wasn't the only time my religious and gay identities could have faced off, but didn't. In the church, I was surrounded by an abundance of male erotica in the form of paintings and statues of half-naked saints and the crucified Christ. As I was growing up, nothing was ever said about such depictions, but in his book Sanctity and Male Desire, Donald L. Boisvert had plenty to say. From his perspective as a young seminarian aware of his gay identity, Boisvert writes openly about his fantasies, the masculine and erotic undertones of St. Michael with his very masculine wings, the male energy of St. Francis as an activist fighting for the marginalized, St. Joseph filling the Daddy role perfectly, the boy saints and their boyish innocence, and the suffering, semi-nude martyrs with hints of S&M. Ironically, these images ultimately strengthened both Boisvert's sexual awareness and his faith in God and the Church.

Growing up, neither priest nor parent said anything about same-sex attraction. You might suspect that homosexuality would be painted as bad from the very start of my religious upbringing. But in truth, my boyhood memories of religious morality and same-sex attraction draw a big blank. I never thought of religious garments as dress-like. I had never seen sanctified men as objects of male desire. Unlike Boisvert, same-sex erotic thoughts never crossed paths with the sacred images called up by prayers, statues, or Bible stories in my prepubescent mind. Religion was boiled down to an easy set of procedural rules to follow, prayers to recite, and creeds to subscribe to blindly. As long as you confessed your sins, went to Mass, and didn't get a girl pregnant, you were going to heaven. With no understanding of sexuality, religion, and a priesthood rife with predatory members, my gay side and my religious side slid by each other silently like two slippery fish in the sea.

How did my sexual and my religious selves become frictionless and totally separate? I'm sure it was because growing up in a Roman Catholic, Filipino family in the 60s, there were no images to hold up as bad. When half-naked men plastered across magazines and pornographic movies became identifiable objects of evil in the eyes of the morally righteous, fearful parents, especially

The Archangel Michael Defeating Satan, Guido Reni, 1635 [PUBLIC DOMAIN IMAGE]

fathers obsessed with the masculinity of their sons, could point to these images and say, "Don't be like that or I will beat you."

But we lived in a Miami suburb, sheltered from the sexual iniquities of the inner city. The magazines splayed across our coffee table (and beside the toilet) were Newsweek, Liguorian, and Readers Digest. Mom and Dad were embarrassingly naïve about mainstream American culture in general. They were clueless when it came to LSD, the Doors, and Dustin Hoffman in The Graduate. Once when Mom emptied out my little brother's pants pockets for laundry, she found a little plastic bag of fine, dried green leaves. "What is Arturo doing with oregano in his pocket?" she asked me.

In Tagalog, "He loves her" and "She loves her" are the same. Add this linguistic blurring to their naiveté and it becomes easier to understand why we never talked about same-sex attraction. Mom and Dad were oblivious even to the topics of queer uncles, old maid aunts, and "colorful" personalities such as Paul Lynde or Liberace. Flamboyant entertainers were okay and sometimes even welcomed on our TV. But talking about gay love or gay sex was as rare as talking about Ptolemaic astronomy.

I thank God for a silver lining left by this big blank: an escape from the inner conflict between gay urgings and cultural-religious morality. So many other gay men have heartbreaking stories about parents, teachers, and clergy instilling lifelong guilt over same-sex attraction. But in my case, same-sex attraction was not immoral. It was just invisible. The corollary? Soul-searching, painful coming out stories were not part of my gay development. For better or for worse, my life skipped over that gay rite of passage.

Years after my altar boy days, my gay, Filipino-American, sexual, and amorous selves developed a friendly, if not affectionate relationship with God. This relationship took its first form by imagining God as the best version of me I could think of. Now God is an awe-inspiring mystery I take comfort in. And he is my friend.

Justin Estoque retired as executive vice president at the Autry Museum of the American West in Los Angeles and previously from the Smithsonian's National Museum of the American Indian. He has been appointed to the Community Advisory Committee of the American LGBTQ+ Museum (NYC). He serves on the board of VOX Femina LA, California's top women's chorus, leads tours of historical movie palaces for the LA Conservancy, and sings baritone with the Gay Men's Chorus of LA.

Aaron Foxman
and the Postmodern
Torah Holders

By Marc Weiner

I.

1973 STARTED on a Monday. Nineteen days later Richard Nixon was inaugurated for a second term; seven days after that the Paris Peace Accords were signed. At 14 years old I didn't really understand the war, but we'd grown up together. Then, in late October of 1973, I went with my father and Aaron Foxman to our suburban temple to hear a lecture by a famous author, a *New York Times* reporter on a book-tour talking about the men who had dreamed up the Vietnam War. And that night, waiting for the lecture to begin, Aaron said something that for the first time in my life made me realize that it wasn't just me, that apparently a lot of people, maybe everybody, thought about sex more than I'd ever imagined.

II.

Aaron Foxman was everything my father was not: educated, comfortable with tradition and modern culture and, most of all, at ease with himself. He spoke French and played the violin, both fluently. My father's social climbing was to have friends with titles, doctors mostly. Though not a physician, Ron's fluency in foreign language and musical expression made him a desirable friend. My father wanted to be friends with someone spoke who French and played the violin, both fluently. That fact that he and Ron genuinely liked each other was a bonus.

What my father sought was to be in the club. In the grammar of Romance languages, he wanted to engage with men of high degree *en el tuteo, dans le tutoiement,* in the familiar, and that explains why my father invited Ron Foxman to hear David Halberstam at our suburban temple that mid-autumn evening; not that my father wanted to go to the event, but that he wanted to go to the event with Ron. I'm not sure why I wanted to go, but I did.

III.

The temple had Torah holders on either side of the ark, sculptured functional works of art, postmodern, wooden, gracefully carved, oddly well-proportioned. You could easily see the outline of a body: legs wide and muscular at the thighs, straight and stable to the floor; arms upward, stretched open and vulnerable. And where the lap of the wooden body would be, there was an extension—a shelf—where the holy scrolls would sit. Protruding upward from below the shelf at the point where the legs meet, up past the shelf and about a third of the way up the arms, there was—almost without purpose, or perhaps with all too much purpose—a single, thick, curiously-curved, highly-polished, wooden shaft, facing upward at an angle, the furthest point an enlarged knob.

Ron Foxman was just making casual conversation when he pointed at the Torah holder on the right and said to my father, "Well if that doesn't look like an erect penis jutting out from a pair of thighs, then I don't know what does."

I didn't look up from the program I was pretending to read, but my 14-year-old world experienced a sexual earthquake. Ron's casual conversation, his breezy comment, reverberated deeply; I was embarrassed and titillated and—hearing the words erect penis—instantly overcome by a rush of thoughts and images. Immediately the future seemed brighter. It felt good to know that I wasn't the only one who had seen sexual angels in the architecture; I wasn't the only who had noticed that the Torah holder seemed to have a swollen, tumescent penis. I felt connected to Ron. He'd seen it too.

I knew I would have to look at my father sometime, but there, then, with my head down, the secular, the sacred, and the profane merged and, knowing his prudishness, knowing that it would embarrass him more than me, I did my best to not look at him. To this day, I don't know how he reacted; we never spoke of it. But Ron had said the words "erect penis" out loud and there was no going back.

IV.

The last time I saw Aaron Foxman was 24 years later on a Monday night in November of 1997 at my sister Sandy's house. We were sitting shiva for my father who had died the Friday evening before, and Ron and Fay came to pay their respects.

We sat at the kitchen table and Fay and my mother, not yet an Alzheimer's casualty, talked between themselves quietly, in that almost-audible-whisper elderly Jewish women use when they talk about death. Ron and I talked about my father and, among other things, reminisced about our literary moment together nearly a quarter of a century earlier. Neither he nor I mentioned the Torah holders. I believe he'd forgotten them, a discussion that for him had long since run its very short course. To Ron, his candor, his free association, his willingness to speak easily, had not been noteworthy; it had just been his way of life. To me it was a magical boundary-expanding moment.

Marc Weiner is a happily retired professor. Over the years, he has loved and been loved by nine miniature schnauzers. He's also been married to Patrick for three decades and likes to cook. And write.

How My First Online Love Took a Wrong Turn

By Robert Kingett

I WAS ELATED TO FIND my first love in the disability LGBT space—another blind man named Frank. It happened after chores on a Sunday. Skype rang. My screen reader, through my Bluetooth earpiece, told me that it was Frank. I answered it right away.

The banter was like a vice; I was trapped. He was tech-savvy. He was charismatic. And, most of all, he was much older and more attuned to the LGBT space. I knew the disability better than I knew the LGBT world. Up to this point, nobody was interested in me. I was twenty years old at the time.

Now I was in heaven. I got what I wanted from Frank. He'd text me throughout the day telling me that he hoped this event would go well or that editor accepted my article pitch. He celebrated with me when I sold an article and he listened to me vent when I ranted and raved about the political disaster that was capitalism. He comforted me when I wanted to tell him that life wasn't fair, and I gave him advice on cheap adaptive technology that he was going to purchase. This was becoming true love.

I listened for a year when he would get mad at his mother because she wouldn't drive him somewhere—a forty-year-old man with his own booming computer repair business. After a year of talking and stretching our obvious true love to the farthest inch, I bought a Greyhound ticket and left for his state with a small suitcase in one hand and my red-and-white cane in the other, with the backpack that held all my electronic equipment. It didn't matter that nobody knew where I was. It didn't matter that I'd just vanish from classes and the newsroom where I was an intern. I had to embrace this true love. There wouldn't be another chance. Days before my departure, however, Frank kept testing our love by asking me if I'd really do what I said I'd do and come to be with him. He predicted that I wouldn't, but he didn't know how much I valued our love. I'd show him.

I arrived with open arms into his life, and he returned the favor. He showered me with kisses and bubble baths, and he would even help me get dressed in the morning and at night. Frank and I were inseparable. It was true love, after all. He wanted to bask in my presence constantly, even when I wanted some alone time to write. He needed to be with me. He needed to be held by me. Luckily, the laptop was the only distraction. My cell phone didn't work out there where Frank lived. It didn't matter though, because Frank and I were going to get through the good times and the bad, together. We were going to let our true love flourish.

I started to wonder if his love was smothering. I'd want to have space so I could write. He needed to hear me and feel me beside him at all times. He really needed someone to be there beside him, because he didn't have anybody with him at all. I was all he had. He didn't like it when I'd say I didn't want wine, or I wanted to wear headphones when e-mailing someone. He needed to make sure I wasn't getting into trouble on my computer. He'd never hurt me in any way, so I was going to help him drink all of this wine he bought. He was looking out for me. He reminded me that it was what people who are truly in love do. I wasn't sure if this was true love.

Months later, his friend and I started chatting on Facebook. I was doing some writing advice sessions online, and his friend really enjoyed my feedback. Frank became furious that I was talking to him. I explained: "Babe, I'm helping him write his cover letter." Frank stomped around his apartment and kept muttering to himself. He told me that Terrance was a man snatcher and would try to take me away from him. I asked him why he didn't trust my intellect enough to let me judge that for myself.

That was when the strike sent me sprawling on the floor. He told me that I was never to back talk him again. I realized that his kind of love wasn't the kind of love I wanted. That night, I stayed up and packed my bags as Frank slept. Cabs didn't come out there, so I begged his mom to take me to the Greyhound station. She agreed, asking me if the love didn't work out. I didn't know how to answer her.

As I sat on the bus to Chicago, where I now reside, I heard a newly engaged couple gushing about their wedding plans. They were tweeting their excitement and furiously squealing the news to anyone who would listen. I gave them a small smile when they looked at me sitting beside them. I told them how happy I was that they had finally found true love. They asked me if I was with somebody special of my own. I replied: "Not yet, but I know my true love is out there, somewhere."

Robert Kingett is a blind and gay romance writer who writes fiction, where disabled characters live normal lives, and nonfiction that spans the literary scope and encompasses educational essays, funny musings, or empathetic ponderings. Find him online at sightlessscribbles.com.

Taking the Secret
Out of "Open Secret"

By Terry Boyle

FOR MANY YEARS, I taught Irish literature in Chicago, and I would always tell my students: the Irish love to debate, and argue about anything that's not personal. We like to pontificate with the best of them but when it comes to personal matters, we become awkward, uncomfortable, and unusually quiet. So, when it comes to approaching intimate subjects, decorum is required. You do not rush in where angels fear to tread. Instead, you avoid the subject.

For instance, my coming out was not accompanied by a fanfare. There was no great catharsis to be followed up by a rainbow party. I was forty years old and quite happy inside the musty old closet of my own making. When it came to coming out, I simply moved from Ireland and took up residence with my partner Larry in Chicago. Everyone knew, but no one really said anything about the new situation. My father, a very pious Catholic, never suspected that one of his five sons might be gay. The closest we came to having a discussion on the subject happened quite accidentally. We were driving downtown, when all of a sudden, he pointed at a man walking down the street and said, "See him? He's a wee bit gay." When I later told this story to my partner, he said: "You should have asked him, which bit of the man was gay?"

In retrospect, this moment might have been the perfect opportunity for disclosure, but I'm Irish and we don't do that sort of thing. It's too personal. My father died none the wiser about my sexual orientation. But when it came to my mother, that's a different story. She and I never discussed the subject, even though she had stayed at our Chicago home several times. She knew, and I knew she knew, and she knew that I knew she knew. It was an open secret after all.

There's no doubt in my mind that the matter of my sexuality was scrutinized, dissected, and interrogated by the other family members, but never directly with me. Having my domestic setup an open secret among the family worked for me. It meant that there were no embarrassing questions to answer and no awkward silences to quickly fill with mindless trivia. I could navigate my visits back home without fear of confrontation. At least, I thought I could, until one of the last trips back before my mother also passed away.

We were driving home from the casino. She loved a little flutter and, in Irish terms, our spell at the casino was quality family time. Joined by a common hope of winning, we bonded over the one-armed bandits. On the way back, from a not-so-lucky afternoon, we ran into traffic and were slowed to a crawl. Music played on the radio, and we laughed about our misfortune. All seemed good until traffic slowed to a halt. As if on cue, the conversation dropped to a more serious tone.

As soon as Mother started with "I just want you to be happy," my heart started racing. I've never had an anxiety attack, and I'm not claustrophobic, but in those moments the car wasn't big enough for both of us, and my nerves were shot. I was convinced that the prelude to mother's opening comments was inspired by Jerry Springer. For a conservative Irish Catholic, Mother enjoyed the freakish absurdities that Springer managed to find. I suppose I should be grateful to Jerry since against the backdrop of these offbeat characters my being gay must have seemed normal to her.

I desperately tried not to fixate on what she was saying. Watching the traffic lights in the distance, I prayed for a distraction, but none came. I'm convinced God was up there laughing his ass off at my increasing discomfort. Her speech hit a crescendo when she confessed to be disappointed at not having grandchildren from me. It was at that point I wanted to laugh out loud. She already had twenty-plus grandkids as it was. One more from me would not have made her life any easier or fuller.

"I thought you'd get married and settled down with children." I tried to make light of the conversation. "You should be grateful that never happened. There's enough Boyles around to re-populate the world, should they be called upon to do so."

My diversion tactic came to naught. Mother could not be dissuaded from her mission. This was the conversation she had wanted to have for years, and I could not stop her. And given that I couldn't very well push her out of the car, I was forced to accept my fate. As I sat there in my discomfort, I began to understand what an important step this talk was for her. Since it was foreign to our culture to say the things she was attempting to put into words, it was quite a brave thing for her to do.

I can never remember my parents ever being very demonstrative. If they were proud of you or thought well of you, you heard it from a third party. When I graduated with my doctorate, I could tell they were pleased, even if they didn't fully appreciate the achievement. I didn't need them to say anything. They came to the ceremony and that was that. Academic accolades are one thing, but they are not personal. Mother was attempting to unlearn her own cultural conditioning, and all I could do was squirm in my seat.

In what seemed like an eternity, but was most likely only ten minutes, she had surpassed me in her ability to evolve beyond our Irish limitations. I was the one more traveled. I was the smart one. But she was the one more open to change. In those minutes, I knew that it is never enough to live with an open secret.

*Terry Boyle is a retired literature professor. He now lives
with his husband in Cathedral City, California.
https://www.youtube.com/@Derrypoet*

All the Life I've Known

By William McMillan

At that moment, I'm thankful for the small things.

The shower in my motel room heats quickly, so I don't have to be cold, wet, and naked for long. There's excellent pressure, the water blasting out as if from a hydrant, creating a racket that muffles the noise roaring out from my chest. Hard, desperate sobs. Hysterical, high school drama student type sobs, furiously long-lasting, the sort I'd make fun of if an actor made such a commotion. Nobody in real life ever cries like that! Except when they do. I point the shower head to the left just a bit, and the water beats the wall like a drum. I'm not worried someone will hear me. I'm in a corner room, it's late, and it's a weeknight in January. I'm worried how easily I can hear myself, how each swell of grief that works its way up my chest cavity and out of my mouth reminds me of what I've done. The water blasts the tan, acrylic walls of my shower. So much noise, and for that I'm thankful.

Motel soaps are so brittle. The one in the shower cracks as I rub it over my body, through my hair, my armpits. I would have packed my shampoo if I'd been thinking clearly that night, but I hadn't done that. What I'd done was to go out in service that day with my brothers and sisters, fellow Jehovah's Witnesses, my Bible and Watchtower in hand. We were spreading the good news of God's Kingdom. What I'd done was buy dinner for my family that evening, driving off to pick up the food I'd called in. Driving back, I didn't know my cousin had gone in my room and used my computer. That he'd stumbled across the endless (and tragically undisguised) links to gay pornography.

What he'd done between the time I'd left home and the time I got home was tell my family what he'd found. What I'd done when I walked in the door and was confronted was lie. I'd set the food on the table and lied. It was all a mistake. An accident. Satan trying to frame me. Not a single Jehovah's Witness is gay. They can't be. Lies, and more lies. What I'd done was pack up my bags when told I was being thrown out, forgetting my dinner, forgetting my shampoo.

There are nine rows of holes in the drain of this shower. Each row has nine holes, 81 holes altogether. There are 35 years in my life at the moment. Each year has twelve months. 420 months altogether. Hundreds of months of perfecting an image, of hiding, of sharp-cornered lies that have been polished smooth until they feel like the truth. Thirty-five years, all the life that I've known, swirling away with the water down 81 holes.

The water cools, and I turn up the knob. At this moment, my world is three feet by three feet, the length and width of the shower. Beyond me, in the rest of the world, events are already in motion. The congregation will ask why I'm no longer at home. My family will tell them, and they'll tell them why. Homosexuality, they'll whisper, as if the word itself is infectious. They'll be formal about it, perhaps even loving, saying I need mercy, forgiveness. But a sister who was revealed to be a lesbian was expelled, a sister no more. Forgiveness is such a kind word when you mean it. Just a sound from your mouth when you don't. I'll have to leave my congregation, I know. My city's a small one, and I'll have to leave it as well. Probably the state. Far enough to find a new congregation where no one knows me or knows what I've done, where I won't have to hear the sounds of forgiveness.

And then, naked and weeping, a thought: "You could stop if you wanted. Stop lying, stop pretending. You could actually be yourself. You've never been that. Have you thought about that? Everything's out, and everything you could lose, you've lost. All of this could be over. Maybe it's time to be someone else."

I run my hand down my chest, feeling slippery, wet skin. I press my fingers down on my sternum, aware that there's more than just flesh and the bone underneath, but something else, something gentle and fragile. No wider than straw, I feel it run the length of my rib cage, a tiny flicker of light within the darkness that's settled within me. So delicate I don't yet recognize it as hope. I turn off the shower, hand on my chest. The feeling remains.

Maybe it's time to be someone else. I get out of the shower and for a moment, there's nothing to hear but the sounds of my breathing. And I'm thankful.

Will McMillan is a queer writer born and raised in the untamed wild of the Pacific Northwest, where he lives to this day. He's a two-time Best American Essays *notable,* Pushcart Prize *nominee, and* Small Best Fictions *winner. His work has been featured in* Electric Literature, Craft, *and* The Sun *literary journals, among dozens of others.*

Moving

A Russian lesbian is stuck in U.S. immigration limbo. A man from rural Montana figures out what it means to be gay and makes his way to California. A Syrian man who was raped for being gay seeks asylum in the U.S. These stories consider what it means to feel grounded in different times, places, and countries simultaneously, and how this friction destabilizes —but also broadens—our understanding of safety, connection, and responsibility.

Processing Time

By Arina Boyko

THERE IS A VIDEO in my photo gallery that I avoid watching but can't delete. It was taken on my last day in the U.S. The dogs circled in the emptied apartment, playing with each other, as if nothing was happening. My clothes piled up in the open suitcase in the background. In the front—my face, swollen from tears.

It's been 205 days since I last saw my wife and our two dogs. Another thing I try to avoid is counting the days. Sometimes numbers ease you, but not when the number is growing and we can't start the countdown. I don't know when I will see them again.

Most people are puzzled when I tell them that marriage to a U.S. citizen doesn't automatically grant you a U.S. visa or residency. That a marriage makes it more difficult for a non-resident to enter the U.S. because they are no longer a 'desired' type of tourist—with a tie too strong to believe they won't take advantage of the country's hospitality.

So my least expensive option—the marriage-based green card—also happens to be the slowest one. The processing time starts at nine months, but often takes twice as long. That's what I tell them, my family. I state the facts as plainly as possible. I don't want them to feel sorry for me.

Before I started *On the Calculation of Volume: Book I* by Danish author Solvej Balle, I already had enough of those conversations. I rarely brought up the green card with my family or friends anymore, and only talked about the present and the past, not the future, which was put on hold by the U.S. Citizenship and Immigration Services.

On the Calculation of Volume is a series of seven books with the narrator Tara Selter waking up on the 18th of November again, again, and again. She is the only one to register the time loop, when everyone else lives each day anew, their memories of the previous November 18th erased.

I learned about the book from the Booker Prize 2025 shortlist, and the moment I learned about its premise I knew I was team Tara. I, too was stuck, not in time, but in the immigration process, where the status of the case—"pending" or "on hold"—became my version of November 18th.

Tara keeps a journal, where she counts and describes her days. What is there to describe if the same day repeats itself? A lot. The entries consist of mundane observations, registrations of moods and other things that fluctuate in the static world. Balle's matter-of-fact style, rooted in tangible reality even when the subject—time—is as abstract as one could get.

Tara has to retell the story of what happened every morning to her husband Thomas. They spend months piecing together the logic behind the time loop, each time to no avail. Reading those chapters, I imagined the book adapted for the screen by Justine Triet, the director of the 2023 drama Anatomy of a Fall, brilliantly portraying the complexities of a marriage between people slowly drifting apart. Soon Tara gives up and isolates herself from Thomas, who still repeats the pattern of the same day, clueless of the fact that Tara is hiding in the guest room.

Not bringing up the green card meant I had to also cut some parts out of my language—the ones about my wife and our relationships, about the dogs that I have but whom I only see now on FaceTime. The self-censorship was not new to me—I was born in the '90s in Russia, and while I was having sex for the first time, Putin was signing a law to ban LGBTQ+-related topics, criminalizing queerness. Was I isolating myself in a metaphorical guest room, stocking up on canned food and chocolate when I didn't talk about my green card? A whole room is of course better than a closet, but it's still not a home.

When the ones who know about my November 18th ask about it, they refer to it as "situation"—as if it's something singular, and the U.S. immigration system is not a machine that puts lives of thousands of people on hold, or, as Tara identifies that state: "I still have plans. Plans of a sort. Although I don't know if they can be called plans anymore. They are loose and open-ended."

I know that "the situation" is common because I became an avid reader of the USCIS subreddit page, where people post their immigration stories daily. There are plenty of posts that read "FINALLY 10 YEARS GREENED ♥♥♥♥" or "RECEIVED BY MAIL, YOU ARE NEXT!" I have nothing to report, and the further I scroll the more I feel like we exist in different timelines.

I read the entire book in bed. While in the beginning I was comforted by it, by the end it crushed me with a heavy realization: Tara was forever changed by what had happened. She will never be able to come back to her past self. Neither will I.

The immigration process, with its invasive bureaucracy, endless waiting time, interviews and exams—is another exercise in state violence created and maintained by nationalist politicians, obsessed with the protection of imaginary borders. Instead of feeling sorry for me, I want people to see the system that causes us suffering—whether we are going through an immigration process, or being isolated and oppressed in any other ways created by late capitalism.

When I was making a birthday wish at the party, one of my friends whispered in a complete silence: "I know what she is wishing for." Everybody laughed: if you know, you know. Sometimes, as Toni Morrison said, you don't get through life whole, you survive in part. And then I hear Tara's voice in my head: "Maybe there's healing in sentences," a phrase that she repeats over and over throughout the book, and I agree: maybe.

Arina Boyko is a writer, editor, and independent publisher. She holds an MFA in Creative Writing from Northern Arizona University. Her essays have appeared in Queer Migration Zine, NYI Constellations *and* The Gay & Lesbian Review.

We Had to Pretend

By Bella Chacha

This story is based on real patterns of queer survival in Nigeria and real conversations. Names and identifying details have been changed for protection.

THE DAY CHRIS MARRIED Amanda, his best friend of seventeen years, there were no butterflies in his stomach–only the quiet ache of survival. They smiled for the cameras. They cut the cake. They danced to Flavour's love songs while his mother dabbed happy tears with her lace handkerchief. Everyone said they were a match made in heaven. No one knew they had made a pact beneath a sky full of secrets.

In Nigeria, being gay isn't just taboo, it's a criminal offense. It's a life lived under erasure. You can be arrested, disowned, beaten, or worse. The law doesn't just deny you, it gives people permission to hunt you. Growing up in Enugu, Chris learned early to bury his truth deep inside him. His mother, a devout Catholic and a widow, used to remind him constantly: "You are my only son. Your children will keep your father's name alive."

He didn't have the courage to tell her he was gay.

Amanda was the only person who knew. He came out to her during their National Youth Service Corps (NYSC) year of mandatory service, crying into a bottle of beer as she held his hand and told him, "I'll never leave you stranded." At the time, he didn't realize how much weight those words would carry in the years ahead.

The pressure to marry ramped up as Chris approached 35. Aunties came knocking with "intentions." Church elders dropped hints wrapped in Bible verses. His mother began calling more often, worried he would grow old without fulfilling his duty to their bloodline.

It was Amanda who finally voiced the question neither of them had dared to ask: "What if we got married?"

Chris laughed at first, but then they both stopped laughing. The idea made a cruel kind of sense, a camouflage, but it was also a relief, a cover that might finally end the daily pressure and intrusive questions. Amanda had no desire for a traditional marriage either. "I'm not built for that kind of life," she'd said once. "But I can love someone with my loyalty."

So, they planned the wedding.

They moved into an apartment in Lagos. They posted carefully curated photos on Instagram–of them in matching outfits, filtered beach selfies, casual videos of cooking jollof together. The illusion was perfect. Chris's mother rejoiced. Neighbors praised their "beautiful union." Meanwhile, the two of them lived as housemates and allies, building a shared world built on truth behind closed doors and performance outside it.

Then came the matter of children.

In Nigeria, two or three years of marriage without pregnancy is enough to invite gossip, unsolicited prayers, and deep suspicion. The whispers can be louder than any siren: "Is she barren?," "Is he impotent?," "What kind of marriage is that?"

Amanda expected these questions. And each time, she defended them both.

She chose a donor—a friend, discreet and emotionally unattached—and she got pregnant. Only they knew the arrangement. When the baby arrived, Chris's mother wept with joy. "My first grandchild, my blessing and my bloodline" she cried, dancing barefoot in the hospital hallway. Two years later, Amanda had a second child, and the circle of protection widened.

I met Chris through a mutual friend, and over time, he opened up about his situation. He wasn't looking for pity, just space to breathe. As I listened to him, I realized how many layers of bravery their story held. This wasn't just a survival strategy. It was an act of quiet rebellion. Two people refusing to be broken by a society that sees their existence as shameful.

Sometimes, he told me, he lies awake wondering what it might feel like to live openly. To hold the hand of the man he truly loves. To explain to his children someday that their father isn't sick or sinful, just hidden. But this country is not yet ready for that truth.

Chris and Amanda's story is not an isolated one. There are many like them—men and women forced into cover marriages to escape violence, rejection, or social extinction. Some do it with sorrow. Others, like Chris and Amanda, do it with friendship, loyalty, and a quiet kind of hope. They are not deceivers. They are architects of survival, crafting homes in the cracks of a hostile world.

Sometimes I ask myself what would happen if Nigeria chose compassion instead of condemnation. If we allowed our queer brothers and sisters to live and love freely. If mothers like Chris's could embrace their sons without demanding they abandon their truth.

Maybe one day that will happen.

Until then, people like Chris and Amanda will keep building lifelines where others see dead ends. They will keep showing us what love can look like—even when it has to hide.

Bella Chacha is a Nigerian writer whose work explores myth, memory, and transformation. Her stories have appeared in Incensepunk Magazine *and* Cosmic Daffodil Journal, *and she was the runner-up for the 2025 Defenestrationism.net Short Story Contest. A Pushcart Prize nominee, she has work forthcoming elsewhere.*

The Closet Is My Country

By Damisola Sulaiman

How do you accept that your closet is a country, that the place that made you into the person you are, is where you can't be yourself?

Immigration is difficult enough when you're searching for a better life and know that there's no hope for that in the place you came from, and when paired with a search for safety in a home country that offers a life of repression and danger, it takes on an added layer of difficulty.

I left Nigeria at eighteen years old to get my university degree. Many factors went into the decision—a better education, improved career prospects, a more structured system, and countless other opportunities. Getting to live freely in my queerness was not a factor I took into consideration, but it's one of the strongest reasons behind my secret desire to leave.

Growing up in Nigeria, even my earliest exposure to queer representation was paired with homophobia. When I was about six years old, a clip of Britney Spears and Christina Aguilera kissing appeared in a recap show of important moments from MTV's Video Music Awards. My mum said, with more repulsion than I'd ever heard her exhibit, "They're going to burn in hell fire."

My mum's reaction to that kiss was only the beginning of the homophobia that was pushed on me for the rest of my childhood and adolescence in Nigeria. From that first moment to the day I moved, I couldn't escape hatred for queer people.

When same-sex marriage was legalized in America in 2015, everyone from family to teachers talked about how America was the devil's playground and a disgusting place for letting queer people live freely. At nearly every religious service I attended, leaders would find a way to work homophobia into their sermons.

All I desired at the time was to belong and to be just like everyone else, so I joined in on the hatred, pushing my truth to the back of my mind. When arguments about the basic human rights of queer people were brought to the table, I was part of the 'I don't think any harm should come to them, but I disagree with their lifestyle' brigade. I clung to religion whenever my own desires came to the surface.

I avoided any moments that highlighted my true feelings with rigor. The friends I wanted to spend every waking moment with were just people I cared about platonically. The women I lusted after was just a person I admired because of her objective beauty. I internally reinforced the religious messaging I was told my whole life.

But the same religious messaging I pushed myself to internalize was also used to justify the violence against queer people, and even at my highest points of denial, I couldn't find a justification for that. My more feminine male peers in boarding school were bullied aggressively, with slurs hurled at them and were constant victims of humiliation. There was also a barrage of videos of gay men who were found in different parts of Nigeria and subjected to all sorts of brutality that went viral on a regular basis.

When I got to my mid-teens, I had enough exposure to unlearn some of the ideas I was socialized with, and eventually, I started to poke holes in the dominant rhetoric. Violence is never acceptable but when queer people are the recipients, the perpetrators are doing God's work? Everyone is equal in the eyes of God but not people in the LGBTQIA+ community? My questions were incessant, and every religious leader I posed them to failed to provide me with real answers; I was often told God would make it clear to me, I just had to keep the faith.

By the time I had finished sixth grade and my departure from Nigeria was imminent, my doubts were at an all-time high, and my faith withered with the more investigations I carried out. The #endsars protests in October 2020 were a massive moment of truth for me. Nigerian youth all over the country protested the police brutality they had been subjected to by the Special Anti-Robbery Squad and rallied together for the first time to stand up against our corrupt government's enabling of violence. I was inspired that my fellow young people could be hopeful for my country after all.

During the movement, queer people also took to the streets to say enough is enough for the violence they had been subjected to at the hands of SARS, and Nigerians turned against them. The narrative was that if liberation involved queer people, it wasn't worth having. It was a harsh reminder of how deep this hatred went and as my own feelings became more unavoidable, I started to realize that there was likely no place for me to exist fully in the place I'd called home.

Being a bisexual woman gave me a lot of space to avoid truths about myself throughout my adolescence in Nigeria but when I left for England, the truths bubbled to the surface as though they could sense they had the space to be freed.

My turning point came without my knowledge. Suddenly, I spoke openly about my desires to friends and gradually changed my appearance to match the way I had always felt. The doubts I had about religious justifications for cruelty toward queer people crystallized into a lack of faith entirely. I let go of purity culture and internalized homophobia, and was the freest I had ever felt in my life. When I built my own community of queer people, I felt bathed in an understanding of solidarity that I had been missing. As more time passed, I leaned further into my identity and could no longer imagine returning home permanently.

When I finished my degree, conversations about what I wanted the rest of my life to look like suddenly came up from so many angles, and it became apparent to me that going back to Nigeria was never going to be an option. The state of the country plays a massive role in this, but many of my friends felt that despite Nigeria's difficulties, they could build their careers in the UK and eventually go back to live in Nigeria. But for me, and a lot of my queer Nigerian friends, this could never be the case.

After working so hard to push out of the mental boxes from growing up in a highly conservative and homophobic system, it seemed almost ridiculous to subject myself to the pain of existing in those systems ever again and in making that choice— there's so much that must be given up. I had never felt my race until I arrived in England and I had never really thought of myself as a minority. Growing up as part of a majority tribe in the most populous African nation shielded me from racist experiences. I was sheltered by my privilege and coming to England changed me because it became a fundamental part of my reality.

Having a world that was built for me was another benefit I took for granted. When I went out in Nigeria, I never had to wonder if I would be welcomed in a space, if the food would be catered to my palate, or if the music would be enjoyable. I could move freely with the understanding that no matter where I went, it was made with people like me in mind. That hasn't been the case in England, as there is a constant need to double check whether a space is for me before I can even feel safe enough to step in.

Then there's the family aspect. Knowing that my parents, the two people who love me the most in the world, aren't here to make my life easier in the way they did for my first eighteen years, is probably the hardest part of it all. It's the little things, like having someone to drive your stuff to your new place when you move, knowing there's a place where you can always eat your comfort food for free, or sinking into your mum's arms after a difficult day.

Each day, I'm aware of everything I'm giving up, and while queerness isn't the only motivator, it's the one I can't seem to shake. I don't know that I could ever belong in a place where violence towards queer people is met with celebration. Sometimes it feels like choosing between being Black and being queer, but it's not. Because while racism persists in the UK, the system does not explicitly encourage cruelty towards Black people the way that Nigeria's system does to queer people.

As my first visit to Nigeria in years draws closer, I already find myself struggling with the fact that I'll likely need to mask certain parts of myself and it's confronted me with the fact that I'm not as 'out' as I've thought myself to be. ▦

Damisola Sulaiman is a London-based Nigerian culture journalist. Her work has been published in The Dial Magazine, New Lines Magazine, Naked Politics, *and several others.*

About Time: Coming Out on National TV

By Garrett Glaser

"**Garrett**, you're coming out today."

It was December 5th, 1994, almost thirty years ago. First thing Monday morning, and not what I was expecting. The person making that declaration, calmly and with a smile, was my boss' boss, someone I very much liked, Carole Black, the president and general manager of the big, important TV station where I worked, KNBC-TV Channel 4 in Los Angeles. Owned by NBC, it has the second largest TV market in the nation: 48,000 square miles of coverage area in five counties, with an audience of more than nine million.

I was considered "talent," appearing on the station's Channel 4 News each weekday afternoon, anchoring the four minute "Show Business" news segment. I worked hard to get the gig, spending nineteen years in TV newsrooms around the country. I figured I'd eventually bring up the idea of coming out to upper management at Channel 4, but not right away. I didn't want to push too hard, I'd already pissed off a number of news managers earlier in my career for all kinds of reasons; usually, I was too vocal with my opinions about their ideas.

"They're not interested in your judgments about their newscast," a friend reminded me when I worked in Virginia. Ever since, I made it a point to keep opinions to myself and remain on my best behavior.

That's when the *Los Angeles Times* called:

"Hi Garrett. We want to profile you as one of the few out, gay TV news people in the country."

"Great," I said, thinking that I could use the publicity. Maybe it would raise my name recognition, or get me a raise on my next contract. So, I said, "Let's do it!"

When the *Times* story appeared, it couldn't have been better; it was complimentary to me and the station. But a small point made in at the end of it, as if an afterthought, struck a nerve at the station: "Even at KNBC, Glaser has only been allowed to hint at his orientation on air by using the word 'us' instead of 'them' when covering the gay community."

I never brought up the subject of an on-air disclosure to NBC, so station executives had nothing to prohibit. I always figured it was inappropriate for any reporter to make themself a part of the story they were covering; that's how I was educated. I always felt, and still do, that personal disclosures of any kind within a newscast have to be made sparingly and carefully. Context is everything.

A few days after the profile appeared, the newspaper's Calendar section had, almost playfully, launched a tiny, recurring blurb on its TV page. Just a few words, asking, "Is Glaser Out Yet?" NBC, aware of its reputation as a diverse and tolerant workplace, was getting tired of the ribbing. Who could blame them?

And three months after the profile was published, the station president asked me to come out on the air as soon as possible.

And so, with management's full buy-in, on that afternoon's Channel 4 News broadcast, I worked my coming out announcement into one of the news items I happened to be reading that day. It was a short note on the death of the founder of the Pediatric AIDS Foundation, Elizabeth Glaser (no relation): "As a gay man who's lost more than a few friends to the virus, I am grateful to Ms. Glaser [no relation] for helping to heighten awareness of AIDS outside the gay and lesbian community."

Two days later, on December 7th, 1994, the *Times* reported on my official coming out. It was a short piece titled "Glaser Comes Out," confirming that I was finally and fully out to hundreds of thousands of Channel 4 News viewers.

What happened at NBC was proof that one never stops coming out. I knew since adolescence that coming out would be a lifelong process. We make the decision to come out to others all the time, typically weighing the positives and negatives before we choose to do it, if we do at all. It is a risk, but a calculated risk. When I was growing up, even in New York

City, the answer was almost always, "No way. I cannot come out to this person." Simply saying, "I'm gay," or "I'm a homosexual" was enough to get you legally fired, thrown out on to the street by your family, or something much worse.

I always knew how fortunate I was to spend most of my professional life as an "out of the closet" gay man. I worked my way up the ladder for almost two decades in New Jersey, Indiana, Michigan, Virginia, Florida, New York, and California. Certainly, my newsroom colleagues always knew I was gay, but before the *LA Times* called, I never thought about outing myself on the air during a live newscast. The challenge became integrating that kind of personal revelation into coverage of the news on any given day.

Whenever I needed a reminder of what things were like before Stonewall, I only had to recall my 1982 interview with a Pentecostal minister in Virginia Beach. He told me that the Bible decreed that all homosexuals must be put to death, and he was serious. I chose not to come out to him at that moment, although it certainly would've made for a good anecdote. It just so happened that I was in a hurry to get my story on the air that day; ironically, it was about free speech.

Despite moments like that, I always tried to live openly and honestly wherever I worked and lived. Coming out to co-workers could not only get your fired, and legally fired, it could also get you beaten up. Violence against "fags" was treated as a joke in many newsrooms. A friend of mine anchoring in Lansing, Michigan, in those days was told he was being let go because "this station will not have a sexual deviate hosting our newscasts."

I have been in and out of the closet since 1965, when I was twelve years old, entering the eighth grade. That was four years before Stonewall, when being out was rare, even in New York.

When I started in the news business, gay people simply weren't allowed to be open and honest about themselves. We were still forced to hide. Homosexuality was illegal in 49 of the 50 states. In 1967, the year that I came out to my mom, I was 14.

My first job in radio, right after graduating from college, was in 1975. In those days, fag jokes in newsrooms were the rule, not the exception. And I never felt safe enough in those days to challenge the people telling those jokes.

All these years later, I realize that's the takeaway: A news reporter can come out on television these days and not lose his job. Newsgathering is a vastly different industry from the one I entered 48 years ago. I hope entry-level reporters today are aware of that and remember it.

Coming out is almost never easy, but the stakes are different now. Out still isn't cool in many newsrooms and, without a doubt, it still takes guts, but the days are over when homophobes can fire you outright or get you thrown out of your apartment just because you told them the truth.

I've been retired since 2009, but I know that TV news reporters are now actually encouraged to come out, even in small, conservative markets. Newsroom managers now want openly gay journalists on their teams, and not solely to improve their coverage of the lives of their gay viewers. Finally, after decades of pain and fear, the business seems to really understand that reporters do better work when they live as their authentic selves. It's about time.

Garrett Glaser published his memoir, Fairyboy, *in 2025. He was a news anchor, correspondent, and producer for 30 years at CNBC, ABC, NBC, CBS, and* Entertainment Tonight, *and in 1994 became the first on-air local news talent to come out publicly.*

A Syrian Story Comes to the U.S.

By Musbah Shaheen

WHEN I WAS FIFTEEN years old, I was raped by two men. I was living in Syria where I was born and raised. I met the two men on some obscure chat room. I remember getting into a car to go somewhere and getting in a car to go back home. The rest is a blur. I don't remember many of the details of that night. I do remember going home feeling okay. I wasn't upset, I wasn't scared, I wasn't in pain.

This was my first sexual experience as a gay man. Part of me thought: "This is what's supposed to happen." Most gay people in Syria don't have many role models of healthy relationships growing up; I certainly did not. I learned to be gay in a country where the law would not protect me when my body was violated, but would be more likely to punish me. Homosexuality is a crime in Syria. Despite the risks, I was so confident in my identity and so desperate for intimacy that I "dated" people who were bad for me, stayed in toxic relationships, and tolerated behavior from intimate partners that I would not tolerate now (at age 26).

I moved to the U.S. for college, got a BA and an MA, and then started my doctorate. Over the last six years, I have realized that this is where I want to be. This is where I need to be to be safe, and to succeed. This is also where I need to be to have fulfilling and healthy relationships, to date, to fall in love, and to do what makes me happy. So, I started to actively pursue asylum in the U.S.

Seeking asylum was one of the most difficult processes I have ever gone through. The most important part is the interview. You have to prove that you have a legitimate fear of returning to your country. The more details you can add to your story, the more likely you are to be considered for asylum. You sit in a room with complete strangers and tell them your deepest and darkest fears. You meet with a total stranger, a lawyer, and answer their questions: "What have you experienced in the past? Are you afraid? What are you afraid of?"

Then you write your personal statement, which is another important part of the process. It turned out they needed to have me prove that I'm gay, which I found to be very amusing. I jokingly asked: "Well, I don't have a gag reflex—does that work?" The lawyer said no. I wrote about the first time I realized I was gay, and my first sexual experiences with those two men.

There was a heavy air in the room as the lawyer asked me to elaborate on what happened, how it felt, and what I did. I had buried that night for so many years, but at that moment it all came rushing back. The smells, the feeling of the couch, the pain, the breath of the men, the shame. So much shame! The lawyer looked at me and said: "That sounds like rape." I laughed through my entire interview, giggling like a bonehead. As I told the stories, I did not use the word rape. My lawyer was taking notes and wrote on the margins "rape," and then underlined it three times. If anyone had told me this story, I would have thought of it as rape. Why had I never thought of it as such? Why did the word 'rape' feel so heavy?

I think part of me always perceived an assault as an event; it occurs at a specific moment in time and then ends. I came to realize that trauma is much more insidious; it goes under your skin. It's in the back of your mind telling you things about yourself, about the people around you. It whispers thoughts about your worth, your image, how you're perceived in the world. I have been carrying my rape with me for ten years. It showed up in every failed relationship, every hookup, every trip to a gay bar, every time I logged on to Grindr. My initiation into sexual life was nonconsensual, coercive, and illegal. I was raped.

I used to tell people that my life was turned upside down when I realized I was gay in Syria. Part of me always blamed being gay for the hard times: the insecurities, shutting people out, losing family and friends, losing my home. But maybe it isn't being gay but how others forced me to give up my body agency, to be a mere sexual object, to be submissive, and to feel like "I asked for it."

My asylum case is still pending, so the future is still uncertain. Part of the healing process is acknowledging what happened, and today I'm taking another step toward healing. So. here's to coming out for a second time: I am a survivor of sexual assault.

For victims of sexual assault, call RAINN.org's National Sexual Assault Telephone Hotline at 800-656-HOPE (4673).

Mushah Shaheen is a queer Muslim, born and raised in Syria. He is an academic researching and writing about college students' religious and sexual identities.

Young and Gay
in Montana

By Scott Terry

I REMEMBER THE DAY in eastern Montana, 1984, when I first understood that I could be killed for being homosexual. Being gay wasn't an existence for me yet, but I knew who I was. I had little hope for experiencing it. The rural cowboy town I called home had a population that hovered around 4,000. Ninety-five percent of its residents identified as white, and one hundred percent were assumed to be heterosexual.

I was still rodeoing, but had given up bull riding. During hunting seasons, a hunting rifle was hanging on the gun rack in the back window of my truck. Being murdered didn't seem likely, if I could successfully conceal that I was gay. If unsuccessful, ostracism was a certainty. Gay men and women didn't survive small-town life in the American West without fear.

Not that I had any hopes of meeting a man like me. I was certain that there were no other gay men like me. I had been indoctrinated in the belief that all gay men wore women's clothes, and that most lived in San Francisco or Hollywood. I desired what I knew, which was a rural, masculine man who could do physical things and lift heavy objects; a man who could get dirty, who could kill his own deer; a man like me, who desired another man like me; a man who I did not believe existed. I even questioned how I could possibly be homosexual.

That year, at 20 years old, I drove to the city of Billings to visit an eye doctor who could dispense contacts. There were no optometrists in my town. Unexpectedly, I discovered an adult bookstore. I went in, of course, hoping to see something, anything, that showed a man with his clothes off.

The bookstore's selection of gay magazines was shockingly more extensive than I had imagined; I perused many. One showed men hanging out in a rural irrigation ditch, wearing leather paraphernalia that I could neither identify nor find purpose for: leather armbands, leather strappy things that went over their shoulders, chaps without pants. The only leather I owned, other than cowboy boots, were my bull riding chaps. I assumed the men in the magazine were bikers, like Hells Angels, except they didn't look like Hells Angels. They were clean-cut and toned. I didn't find them particularly erotic. I couldn't imagine any purpose for their leather accoutrements, or why a gang of motorcycle riders needed such things. I just wondered how a gay porn magazine had convinced a group of bikers to hang out naked in an irrigation ditch.

I bought an *Advocate* magazine and scoured its contents. Most stories focused on the urban lives of gay men and women who had the nerve to be visible, and it referenced gay life in cities like San Francisco and Hollywood; but I failed to connect with anything it printed. It did not represent me.

It did have a massive selection of personal ads, organized by state. While there were none from Wyoming or Montana, where I had grown up, it gave me a glimmer of hope. This is how gay men could meet, apparently— through ads in the Advocate personals.

A few weeks after I posted an ad, I received a phone call from Dan who was a cattle rancher in North Dakota. He was in his thirties, single, and lived on the ranch that had been in his family for generations. His brother was married with children and his parents were still alive. All resided on the ranch property. Dan called me around midnight.

That made sense to me. Gayness belonged in the dark, I thought. Neither Dan nor I had ever fully consummated sexual activity with another man. I received two midnight phone calls from him.

Weeks later, I found the nerve to call him back at dinner time. I had to remind him of our previous telephone discussions of sex. He claimed that he must have been drinking. I never called him again, and wouldn't pursue a man who could only be gay when drunk.

I soon drove back to the Billings bookstore when I realized it was a safe place for men to meet men. That's how I met Al. Rugged and masculine with a fantastic moustache, Al worked in the oil fields, like me. He had grown up in the little town where I lived, but had moved to Billings a decade earlier. He had left our town, he said, when he became certain that he would either be killed, or his parents' home would be burned down, if he stayed. The same would happen to me, he said, if I didn't get out.

Al came back to visit his parents a few weeks later and spent a half hour in my basement apartment. He was uncircumcised, and felt the need to disclose this before we took our clothes off. I had the barest inkling of what that meant. Apparently, he said, some gay men didn't like uncircumcised penises. I wasn't one of them. The thought that there could be any preferences for penis specifics hadn't yet occurred to me. I was dumb as a post, when it came to sex. He embraced me when I shook with fear for what we were doing.

Al and I never spoke, or met, again. I was too young. Too inexperienced. Too terrified. Too risky, for him.

In that same year, a man who was neither a cowboy nor of a rural background, arrived in town and opened a hair salon. His shop always seemed empty. He had no customers that I was aware of. I went in for a haircut, just once, and decided that he was most definitely gay. Perhaps he wasn't. What the hell did I know? He seemed slightly effeminate, to me, light in his loafers, as I would later hear a man like him described.

Men of that type did not exist in cowboy country. If this man was a homosexual, he needed to be more invisible, like me, I thought. I worried I could be seen by friends as I left his place of business.

He lasted less than six months. His storefront was soon emptied and I assumed he abandoned our town because he didn't feel like he belonged. As would I. In 1985, I sold my horse and moved to California. The lies and maneuvering it would require to exist in eastern Montana didn't seem possible. I had turned 21 and couldn't imagine any form of life that could exist for me, there.

A few years later, I met Lee Kittelson at a rodeo in California. Lee had grown up in eastern Montana, only thirty miles from where I had once lived. He had also moved to California, and we roped together for a couple of years.

Lee died during the AIDS epidemic, and it's been forty years since my phone call with the rancher in North Dakota who could only 'be gay' when drunk. I've thought of him often since then. What was a man like him to do? Be the first generation in his family to leave the ranch and move to San Francisco? What kind of courage, or desperation does it take for a rural man who only knows agriculture and ranch life, to leave? Did he ever find it?

Today, if asked, I would describe myself as a happily-married gay man who raises great tomatoes and melons on my farm. I shot a nice buck last year, and I can still handle a rope just fine when branding calves. I no longer think I need to be invisible, nor do I live in fear, but I had to leave rural Montana to get to that place and meet someone new along the way.

The author in 1987.

Scott Terry is an organic farmer and cowboy in California who writes fiction and nonfiction. His books and rodeo gear are in the permanent collection of the Autry Museum of the American West (Los Angeles).

When My Mother Ran Away from Home

By Wade Rouse

"**I'm on a greyhound bus,** I'm callin' from a pay phone in Rolla, Missouri, and I'm comin' to see you." The accent was as thick as Ozarks molasses. I knew immediately it was my mother. "I want to see you," she said. "I want to meet Gary."

This was decades ago, just before Mother's Day, when I lived in St. Louis. Hearing my mother utter this was the shocking equivalent of picking up the phone to hear Meryl Streep say, "I want to star in the movie based on your book."

I had come out to my parents months earlier and my rural father had disowned me. After we spoke, he sent me a letter that essentially ended our relationship. I had spoken to my mom only a couple of times over the past few months, in her clandestine calls from work, in which she had told me my father was forcing her to choose between me and him. I was anticipating a motherless Mother's Day, which was excruciating for me.

"What about dad?" I asked.

"He was not willing or able to come with me at this point in time," she said. "I cannot live another second of my life without my only son in it. I cannot live another second of my life with regret. Life is as short as one blink of God's eye. It will be over before I know it."

I started to cry. My mother was running away from home.

As we drove to the bus station, my mind wandered to my childhood.

It was not easy growing up a gay boy in rural America in the 1970s and '80s. I preferred ascots to overalls, reading to hunting. And yet, my mother taught me to embrace being different, to use the voice and gifts I'd been given, to relish my uniqueness. Her fierce love likely saved my life, especially after my brother was killed in a tragic accident at the age of seventeen, when I was only thirteen. "You must live," she told me when she left me at college, "so I can live."

My mother was a nurse and, later in her career, a hospice nurse. She was the Florence Nightingale of our rural town, caring for the wounded and the weak, the lost and hopeless. I accompanied her all over the Ozarks—across creek beds and railroad tracks—to care for those at the end of their lives. She taught me that those at the end of their lives were filled with regrets, things they should have done and said. "Don't ever live your life with regret, Wade," she used to tell me.

When Gary and I picked her up, I was petrified. Would she like Gary? Would she still love me?

In the first few seconds of her high-stepping it off the bus (my mother walked at the same speed and with the same gait as a turkey), Gary, a hugger, reached out and grabbed her, holding her body tightly.

"I thought he would be older," my mother said, looking at me. "Your father said Gary would be a much older, wily gentleman, perhaps in his late fifties."

"No, he's younger than me," I replied. "Despite what dad believes, I was not coerced into being gay. I wasn't seduced in a back alley. I've known forever."

"Well," my mother started. "It is nice to meet you finally. Yes, yes, that is correct. Nice to meet you, sir." I had warned Gary about my mother's nervous talk, filled with tics and odd tales, but he was charmed. "I love your voice," he said. "Very *Steel Magnolias*."

I held my breath, but my Ozarks mom smiled at Gary, finally embracing him back.

For the next hour, my mother—whose stories always walked a fine line between fact and fiction—told Gary a fictionalized tale about the life of Shirley MacLaine, who, I know for sure, did not star in *Funny Girl*. She also proceeded to tell Gary about how she believed that, in previous lives, she was Clara Barton, a lioness, and a blind cobbler, not necessarily in that order. Gary told my mother he believed he was an Egyptian goddess, Russian dancer, and close relative to Suzanne Somers, definitely in that order.

I told both of them that I was in hell, but neither laughed because they had already bonded, talking and laughing, like long-lost friends who had reconnected. Despite all of our family drama, there would be no more fights, no anger, no personal drama. That's the thing when you stop judging and start loving, accepting, and understanding. You are more aware, you live in a place of light, you move forward, not back. No, my mother immediately adored Gary, and he adored her back. Gary and Geri were, in short, a match made in heaven.

By jumping on a Greyhound, my mother made a stand that changed my life, Gary's life, and the life of my father—who eventually came around not only to accept but to love me and Gary, largely because of my mother's strength. Over the last 26 years that Gary and I have been together, his parents have given me wonderful gifts my parents could not, and my parents gave Gary things his parents could not.

As we celebrate Pride month, we all must continue to make a stand for what matters in life, regardless of the consequences. When we do, lives are changed, sometimes dramatically, for the better. When we don't, things remain the same, or get even worse. My mom's love for and pride in me, and her show of strength when everything could have been lost for her, changed countless lives and continues to have a ripple effect. She lived without regret, as do I do.

My mother passed away in 2009, but when I am down and need a sign of strength and pride—especially in light of all the vitriol in today's world—I think of my mother buying that bus ticket, jumping on a Greyhound, and running away from home.

Wade Rouse is the USA Today, Publishers Weekly, *and #1 internationally bestselling author of 18 books, including five memoirs and 13 novels (written under the pen name Viola Shipman, as a tribute to his Ozarks grandmother). Wade's books have been translated into nearly 30 languages and selected multiple times as "must-reads" by NBC's* Today Show, Indie Next Picks, *as well as Michigan Notable Books of the Year. Wade's latest novel,* That's What Friends Are For—*inspired by the classic TV sitcom* The Golden Girls— *follows four aging gay men who live communally in Palm Springs and marks the first novel under his own name.*

New Logic

By Caitlin Hanratty

I AM SITTING IN A BOOTH at the Olive Garden across from my mother, but it doesn't look like her. Her voice is still raspy and sweet, with the Long Island Jewish accent that sang me lullabies as a kid and growled at me as a teen. She smells the same, too—a combination of potting soil, patchouli-scented lotion, and zucchini bread. I've never been more comforted by these little, unchangeable details as I look at the stranger who calls herself Darlene.

"I suppose your father told you," Mom says.

"No," I reply. "Dad cried before he could finish his sentence. Then he told me to ask you, which I have a feeling I don't want to do," I add. She's distant and moody, often in her own world and less in mine. She's flakey and off her game. She's keeping secrets. I don't know what they are, but they are as large as the air is heavy between us.

"We're getting a divorce," Mom says. A lingering silence accompanies my blank stare. Suddenly, the endless breadsticks and salad manifest into a new, endless purgatory, trapping me between my need to fall apart and the room of strangers surrounding me. I resent her for fencing in my meltdown.

"Why?" I ask.

My eyes are watery, and through blurred vision I look up and see the waitress drop off our dinners. She's all smiles, so I try to contort my face into something that resembles one, too. I can't even feign the most basic human interaction: a fake smile to match her fake smile.

"Because I'm gay," she adds.

"That's why?" The wheels begin to turn, and the puzzle pieces fall into place. "Is it Annie?"

"You knew?" Mom asks.

"Mom, as far as I knew you and Dad had the perfect marriage. All of my friends think the same; you're everybody's role model couple. You never fought, you got along, and I know you had a good sex life because I could hear you; I'm a light sleeper. Were you faking it?" Where am I getting the nerve right now?, I think to myself.

"Excuse me?" She chokes on her water.

"Were you faking being straight all this time?"

I realize these are deathbed questions. One question leads to five, and soon enough they become unanswerable anyway. Does my being stem from deception, not love? If my mother lived honestly, if she didn't fear judgment from her own mother, if society gave her a softer place to be herself, would I be me? Would I be at all?

"I always knew I wanted kids. Back in the '70s you had to get married to have kids. I knew I had an inkling, but I did, and still do, love your father. That's why making this decision was so hard. He's my best friend," she says. "I'm terrified of losing that. Mostly, I'm terrified of hurting him."

I was hoping to get a yes or no answer, but I realize now it wasn't a yes or no question. Categories make life easy to understand, but they are imprecise. We do not live in a Manichean world in which everything is safely dichotomous: good/bad, black/white, republican/democrat, gay/straight. Boundaries are fluid, and we are complex creatures. Looking at life any other way is reductive, eventually making fools of us all. Right now, I'm playing the fool.

"Uh huh," I say, nodding along while she explains, but, truthfully, I have no idea what to say. I also don't know how much of this I can bear to hear. Slow-motion trauma. I have a finite threshold for it.

"You don't fall in love with a gender, you fall in love with a person," Mom says.

"Uh huh," I reply, as if it's a universal truth: we fall in love with people as individuals, not their gender. I am following a new logic, though I don't quite understand it.

"It's Annie," I say.

This one is black and white. Annie is my mom's friend at the post office where they work. I think back: what were mere oddities at the time turned out to confirm this new logic, too. Annie saw my school play. I thought that was strange. Next, my mother chopped off her beautiful curls in favor of a shorter style, and insisted on being called her proper name, Darlene. Then she stopped eating carbs, right before she stopped eating altogether. Now, my mom wears a bikini. It's like seeing a giraffe transform into a pony, a pony formally known as Dolly. It was a nickname from birth (it's not her fault she looks like a doll) that sits cast aside, like the shedded skin of snakes, a remnant of a time long gone.

One day at the beach, in her skinny body, Darlene told me that she was bored. She didn't follow through with a reason for her boredom, or maybe I never gave her the opportunity to do so, because I immediately told her to take a class. She took a "pottery class," but she never did bring home anything she made. My idea for self-soothing became her cover, go figure. I didn't know she was a volcano on the verge of explosive I thought she was bored in the way I got bored.

"Yes," she says. "It's Annie."

In the days and weeks to follow, my father sits befuddled on the couch, teary-eyed in his robe, conducting a mental autopsy of his marriage. Occasionally, I interrupt his nightmare with my presence. Darlene isn't home a lot. She's making pottery. When she's home, she's sleeping.

"You're done being raised," my dad says.

"Excuse me?" I reply. "I'm seventeen."

"Your point?" Dad asks.

I am surprised he doesn't pull out a cigarette at that very moment. Somehow, a cigarette feels like the right prop to match my newly careless father. But as a runner, smoking is the last thing that he would ever do. But telling me I am done being raised feels just as out of place. How could he abandon me at a time like this?

"I don't know anything. You're smarter than me. Go live your life. Don't let this ruin your senior year," he says. Mind you, my father is quite literally the smartest person I've ever known. He's been deflated.

"You're telling me I don't have a curfew? I don't have to come home? Are you sure? Dr. Phil would say I need structure," I respond.

"As far as I'm concerned, we're roommates. And Dr. Phil is a jerkoff," he says.

Enough said.

Four months later, my mom moves out. It is the day after Christmas.

I am left with a sad father who makes me his therapist. I am fairly certain he should be talking to a professional, or at the very least, a stranger. Telling me that he never cheated on my mother is reassuring, but makes my heart ache more. An active sex life? I vomit.

My father is one of my favorite people, though I never tell him this. Sometimes, things go to his head. He is the person from whom I get my irreverent and dark sense of humor, my love for reading, and my eclectic musical taste. When my mom left, I watched him turn to running when he could have turned to booze. And I watched him turn to God when he could have hidden under his bed. My father forgave my mother, and he gave me the blueprint for how to survive with dignity in a world that is less forgiving.

My mother and I were always close, despite this blip in our relationship. Eventually, Annie broke her heart, as affairs often disintegrate into what they always were: a band aid. Today, my mother is with a woman I would proudly call Mom. Now, my mother looks like an appropriately-aged version of the woman who once sang me lullabies. Her hair is often tied back in a long, stringy braid that sits on her right shoulder. She once considered braiding it in dreadlocks, and thankfully grew out of that, too. She answers to Dolly again. She owns makeup, and once in a great while, wears a bra. She is perfection. New mother. New father. New logic.

Caitlin Hanratty is an English teacher in the Hudson Valley, where she serves as the advisor for her school's chapter of the Gay-Straight Alliance.

Pivoting

A butch lesbian at Harvard Divinity School finds freedom by transitioning to manhood. A Black man escapes transphobia in the U.S. while reading James Baldwin off the coast of Africa. A diplomat is kicked out of the U.S. due to HIV stigma in the 1990s. These stories explore the boundaries we cross, and build, to feel connected. We develop strategies for living every day, navigating institutions that jeopardize the ways we live our lives, the children and ancestors we live them for.

Transitioning To (and At) Harvard

By Ty Bo Yule

I HADN'T PLANNED on transitioning at Harvard. No one would choose to invite puberty to graduate school, but I probably wouldn't have finished my degree if I hadn't started injecting testosterone into my thigh in my second semester. Surprisingly, in 2011, an esteemed liberal arts program turned out to be a perfectly comfortable place to renovate my identity. They had great health insurance; and most academics love a fresh opportunity to be culturally sensitive.

I didn't tell the Divinity School they were my exit strategy from the life I was trying to incinerate when I applied. I told them about the queer bar I had opened to provide a sanctuary for my people. I then related my eight semesters of ancient Greek and fascination with Late Second Temple Judaism to my dyke bar prophecy, and they were all in. Harvard Divinity School cultivates diversity, and they had never had one of me before.

By the time I landed at Harvard, I was forty and emotionally and physically exhausted from a lifetime of manual labor, interpersonal conflict, debauchery, and hope. Hope is the most debilitating of these afflictions because it is the relentless belief the world might favor you more warmly if you could only confound and exceed its expectations. This is a fruitless exercise for a woman who looks like they don't want to have sex with men or make babies.

I had lived my whole life as a masculine woman, a butch dyke. Even as a child, my uncommon presentation was unmistakable. In adolescence my sexuality was obvious. In every mundane, daily interaction from my earliest memory, I was a naturally occurring contradiction. I was a circumstance that demanded a response, whether it be curiosity, denial, discomfort, anger, ridicule, or fetishization. Circumstances don't develop a healthy self-perception or even a sense of human entitlement. From my experience, they simply seek to limit risk.

As soon as I could, I moved to San Francisco, where I'd heard there were other people that looked like me. I also found people who thought the way I looked was cute. Clots of rebel affinities used to form freely in cities. These magic bubbles of the marginalized might have broken your heart, but at least there was enough safety for a young ego to start to form. Heteronormative people rarely entered those spaces out of fear. That means the standards for cultural acceptance were set by one's peers rather than dominant society, and the outside world was obscured. I never had to wear a dress again, but I worked overtime at being cool.

When I wanted a less strenuous version of this kind of refuge, I moved to Minneapolis. This is where I opened a queer bar in an effort to preserve the wild enchantment of queer spaces against the encroaching environ-mental forces of normative assimilation in the broader LGBT agenda. Dyke bars across America were dying at the time. Mine died too. I didn't know what else I could do to provide a natural habitat for people like me, so I decided to try something completely different, go someplace I'd never been, which is how I ended up in the Ivy League.

I chose Harvard as a last-ditch attempt to exceed expectations, mine and probably those of my parents. We all needed a win. I wasn't thinking ahead to what the experience might actually involve. I just wanted to see my parents at a graduation party, unable to formulate any clever critiques of my life choices because every Harvard

The author's book about his dyke bar and transition.

degree comes with at least one afternoon of uninterrupted parental restraint.

Preoccupied by this fantasy, I didn't plan ahead. I didn't think about what I was going to wear. I didn't know what classes I wanted to take. I did not anticipate the nature of my future classmates. I assumed I could charm anyone.

I know not everyone who attends Harvard is rich and snobby, but there is a pervasive comfort with comfort. I'd had plenty of practice with people with money, but Marx would have called where I came from the bourgeoisie. My home for the previous twenty years had been the dissident proletariat. As a butch dyke, if you wanted a cute girl to think you were hot, you had to be smart, edgy, and working-class. I spent twenty years driving trucks and forklifts, pretending to understand Kant. I'd owned a bar and drank like a pirate. This blue-collar mystique had been part of why Harvard let me in, but it provided no practical skillset for success there.

I was away from the safety of the fringe for the first time in two decades. I was dressed like a steampunk coal miner when I arrived on campus the first day. I was surrounded by attractive, confident, intelligent people. My costume was my armor. I was minimizing risk again, trying to appear intimidating like a spiked mollusk. And then, everybody was nice. It was damn uncomfortable. I couldn't discern the ingredients of the niceness, but I couldn't help the sensation of feeling like a zoo exhibit. I will admit to half of this impression stemming from insecure emotional projection, but how the hell is an aging pirate to behave when everyone thinks of them as an interesting subculture?

I unraveled. There was no one to fight and no one to protect. This experience suddenly became my responsibility to either master or waste. I wasn't just back in the mainstream world; I was in a rarified version of it. Everyone around me assumed I was a real person with interesting things to say, or they wouldn't have let me in. I didn't know how to be anything but a hustle, and I was exposed and depleted. I gave up on changing the world, so I changed myself.

Testosterone turned out to be better armor. My masculinity is never questioned anymore. I made it through my master's program and impressed my parents and myself. I haven't made much of my fancy degree. I went home and became a bartender who writes things. The normal world is still uncomfortable for me, and I never did get new clothes, but I did find a chance at peace when I got that diploma. It gave me a trump card to deflect any future attack to my self-worth, either from the normative world or my own insecurity.

My transition story is uncommon, but that's why it offers room for a new generation to find value in their own underappreciated triumphs and missteps. Some of us never do it the way everyone else does.

The author at his graduation from Harvard Divinity School in 2012.

Ty Bo Yule is a Gen X, queer, transmasculine writer, teacher, bartender, and comprehensively handy Butch based in South Minneapolis. He is the author of Chemically Enhanced Butch *and recent small-town Pride travel essay series, "Trans Man in a Van: Driving Toward Queer Resistance." Find his witty cultural commentary and pictures of his dog at chemicallyenhancedbutch.com.*

Queer Rain: Reflections on James Baldwin's "Untitled"

By Stacey Nathaniel Jackson

THE BOOK FLAP OF *Notas de um filho da terra* begins: "James Baldwin nasceu em Nova Iorque, em 1924, no bairro do Harlem, onde cresceu e estudou." I purchased the European Portuguese translation of *Notes of a Native Son* on an impulse the day after New Year's 2025, on my way out of Fnac, a store in Madeira. Shops had just reopened. Madeira is a small island in the Atlantic Ocean, an autonomous region of Portugal, closer to the coast of North Africa than mainland Portugal. Fnac didn't have the toner cartridge for my European Brother printer, but I was thrilled to see a sepia book cover of Jimmy on a center aisle, his arm slender, his elbow positioned on top of a Royal typewriter, his ringed hand resting squarely on top of his head, gazing ever so slightly down, away from the photographer's gaze. A pose, no doubt. Pensive. Almost sad, but not.

Translated by Pedro Rapoula, the edition of ten essays was published by Alfaguara "por ocasião do centenário do seu nascimento, celebrado em 2024." Deservedly, the centennial of Baldwin's birth was celebrated around the world, including a festival produced by La Maison Baldwin in Paris, and readings at The Library of Congress in DC, the Museum of the African Diaspora in San Francisco, among others. "Ativista, homem, negro, homossexual…" I thought *Notas* would be a good addition to my small collection of European Portuguese books; I purchased the book-length epic poem *Omeros* by Derek Walcott in Lisbon two years ago.

My wife and I have been planning an escape to a more "neutral" environment for several years, given the MAGA movement's overt attacks on trans kids and adults. From the resurgence of bathroom snoops, sports prohibition, government intervention of puberty blockers, to banning gender-affirming medication for trans adults altogether. Portugal continues to rank high as a friendly LGBT+ travel destination. In fact, discrimination against trans and intersex folk is illegal. Lei da Identidade de Género, the Law of Gender Identity was ratified in 2011. The chance discovery of *Notas de um filho da terra* felt serendipitous, given Baldwin's lived experience, his activism, his fearlessness, and audacity to be his authentic self in life and on the page, in the United States and abroad.

What's less well known is, James Baldwin was also a poet.

His poem "Untitled" begins with one word, one comma, a one-line monostitch: "Lord,".

In her introductory essay to the collection *Jimmy's Blues and Other Poems*, poet and National Book Award winner Nikky Finney speculates, "I believe he wrote poetry because poetry brought him back to the music, back to the rain." In "Playing By Ear, Praying For Rain," Finney makes several references to rain including, "His words fell on us like a good rain." She also wrote, "I had needed Hansberry to set my determination forward for my journey. And I needed Baldwin to teach me about the power of rain."

Analysis of the poem's meaning can be found online, referencing an interview Baldwin gave about the challenges (i.e., pressure) African American artists confront daily, including the need to cater to a White cultural establishment. I haven't read or seen the interview. But here, I am seeing and hearing something else from the poem's narrator.

In fifteen short lines (including four monostiches), I hear a self-reflective prayer compared to Stagerlee wonders, a protest poem, also in the collection. In Stagerlee wonders, the poetic voice is justifiably outraged over the impacts of the Vietnam War, the school-to-prison pipeline, slavery… "Nigger, read this and run!"

From my point of view, the potential to change a future downpour of ponderous rain with a prayer-like spell is the poetic conceit of "Untitled." The biblical connotation of rain cannot be overlooked (e.g., a symbol of God's love), given Baldwin's relationship to religion as a former preacher: But/And. Like all water—bad rain can damage, bad rain can sting, bad rain can flood, and bad rain can kill. Good rain heals, makes things grow, fills reservoirs. Good rain calms.

In his essay "We Are The Stars: Black Speculative Narratives and The History of the Future," John Jennings wrote that Sheree Renée Thomas, editor of *Dark Matter: A Century of Speculative Fiction from the African Diaspora* "…reimagined Black literature as essentially speculative. By doing so, she posited a much earlier origin of Black speculative culture and science fiction that predated the term Afrofuturism."

Which brings me back to Baldwin and "Untitled." What of the falling water? What of the light? What of a different world Baldwin steadfastly conjured in his novels, essays, plays, and poems interrogating race, politics, and sexuality? Is that not the definition of worldbuilding?

My guess is neither Baldwin, Finney, nor previous readers of "Untitled" encountered a Black speculative poem. (Perhaps a non-prayer prayer.) As mentioned, the poem begins with Lord, as in have mercy, or as in Hmmpf, can you believe what girlfriend is wearing? On Instagram, you can watch a video of Billy Porter shimmering in a dress of rainbow sequins, their face fabulously made up in make-up, wearing nose jewelry, reading "Untitled" for their Instagram followers. Evidence Baldwin and "Untitled" will continue to reach new audiences.

I don't talk to god—in prayer or poems. But I do listen to those who do.

Nikky Finney has discussed publicly Baldwin's influence on her poetry. In an interview posted by LitHub's "The Quarantine Tapes" with writer Walter Moseley (an avid supporter of the Black poetry organization Cave Canem), Finney reflects, "It is my responsibility, James Baldwin says, to tell us what it is like to love, what it is like to hate, what it is like to be loved, what it is like to feel hatred for someone, to feel the disillusionment of being whoever we are in the world. That's where I'm going to stand for the rest of my life."

In 2012 at Cave Canem's summer poetry retreat, I eventually felt compelled to come out as a Black-Transman-Praying-I-Was-Passing to Nikky, an out Black lesbian and retreat faculty member at the time. Nikki Giovanni (not publicly out, but who reportedly died with her wife by her side December 9, 2024) was a visiting mentor that summer. Giovanni was another important influence on Finney's poetry. Nikki slipped in late, but surefootedly sat down around the table with us; my poem was up for workshop. Nikki asked flatly about one word, was it the right choice? Did I mean what I wrote? I responded calmly, "yes." After the day's workshop, I realized from hearing several days of feedback and the great Nikki Giovanni's question, that my work made no sense without context. Shyly,

I approached Nikky Finney after a group reading. Told her my truth. "It's all there," she said with compassion and kindness in her eyes referring to my poems, sensing my fragility about outing myself. Her words to me—queer rain.

Stacy Nathaniel Jackson is a trans writer, poet, playwright, and visual artist. His debut novel The Ephemera Collector *was published by Liveright in 2025. His Afrofuturist play* The Codex of Narma *was a semifinalist for the 2025 National Playwrights Conference (Eugene O'Neill Theater Center), and received a staged reading presented by the National Queer Theater, Arts Project of Cherry Grove, and The Other Side of Silence.*

Suddenly Sundered: HIV and the Foreign Service

By Michael Varga

"How soon can you get out of Canada?" asked the administrative officer at the U.S. Consulate in Toronto in October 1995 when I was informed that my application for disability retirement—due to my advanced HIV/AIDS—had been approved.

"What?" I asked.

"Now that you're officially retired, the State Department has liability issues with you remaining in Canada. I need to know how soon you can get out."

He was trying to be kind and not confrontational but nonetheless all I heard were those last two words: get out.

This was the mid-1990s, before treatments became available that extended the lives of those of us with HIV. In 1995, after I pressed relentlessly for a life expectancy number, my doctor had told me that based on my lab numbers and what medications were available then, I could expect to last another eighteen months at most. Things were that grim, with HIV-positive individuals often moving from a first hospitalization to death in mere months.

What no one had prepared me for was the sundering from the Foreign Service when my disability application was approved. A cable had come from Washington on October 20, 1995—four months after I had filed for early retirement—informing the Consulate that my application had been approved. I was told that from that moment on I was no longer permitted in the Consulate building, that I should pack up all my personal belongings and leave the building as quickly as possible.

"You're no longer an employee. The U.S. government has liability issues with you now. You need to get out of Canada as quickly as you can. I don't mean to pressure you. I know you just learned that you're a retiree but the State Department wants me to cable them back when you're leaving Canada." I had no answer. That morning I had been working on a report about some trends at the Toronto Stock Exchange. There was work I still wanted to complete.

I had been HIV-positive ever since the test became available in 1985. The Foreign Service requires a physical examination every two years to maintain worldwide availability to serve as a diplomat. In 1987, when I had my physical exam, an HIV test was conducted, and the Department was informed that I was positive.

I had no symptoms then, and, although there were no medications available to treat the disease, I continued to work like any one else. I had assignments in Dubai, Damascus, and Casablanca. I was good at my job and was promoted rapidly. Still, as a gay man, I had to be careful about my sexuality. At that time, you could be fired for being gay. When my security clearance came up for review in 1991, the security officers told me they knew I was gay, but since I was "closeted," the only way they could renew my security clearance was by interviewing a family member about my sexuality.

I was confused.

"You're at risk for blackmail as a closeted gay man. If someone in your family knows about your sexuality, we can interview them and that removes the threat of potential blackmail." The whole blackmail question was a Catch-22. You couldn't be open about your sexuality or risk being fired.

But they wanted you to be open (at least with someone in your family) so that you couldn't be blackmailed. That weekend, I went home and discussed this with my parents, to whom I wasn't officially out. They said they'd known that I was gay for a long time and had no issue with it. Diplomatic Security personnel interviewed them in the following weeks, and my security clearance was renewed.

I dodged that bullet, but this requirement to hide my sexuality took its toll as I struggled for balance between my working life and my personal life. I could not be open about any relationships, and I couldn't react when other diplomats made jokes about gays, which was often. It was a very unwelcoming atmosphere to be gay in the Foreign Service in the 1980s and '90s.

I am lucky to still be here in 2019. Given what the doctors told me back in Toronto, I had no expectation that new drugs would keep me alive this long. There is only gratitude for that turn of events. But remembering all of those HIV-positive people who never got the chance to grow old (I'm 63 now), I am driven with even more gusto to continue to be of service to others and to share my story.

The State Department was unprepared for how to handle those of us with HIV. In the early days of the epidemic, no one knew how bad it was going to get. So many young lives snuffed out before they had a chance to make a dent in our world. Today there are an estimated 1.1 million of us living in the United States with the virus, and more than 700,000 who died because of it.

I left Canada two weeks after I was told to get out. I had needed time to find a place to ship my things to in the U.S. and to figure out what it meant to be retired, looking my death in the eye. That was a lot to deal with at that time, and a little more compassion from the Department about how quickly an ex-employee could relieve them of their "liability issues" would have gone a long way to making my transition a less harrowing one. ▓

Michael Varga, a retired diplomat, writes fiction, poetry, and essays. His Peace Corps novel, Under Chad's Spell, *is available at Amazon. Please visit his website at www.michaelvarga.com or follow him on Instagram @varga2017a.*

Our Marriage Is Transactional, Our Love Is Not

By Edward Jackson

I **GOT MARRIED TO RIC**, my partner of thirteen years, in the summer of 2019 and moved to a tiny town in Pennsylvania. We had lived together before in Atlanta for over a decade, but he'd gotten tired of the city, while I had not. A job he wanted took him north and I stayed down south. We lived apart for three years and spent copious amounts of money flying back and forth for weekend visits.

By the spring of 2019, I felt that mid-life crisis itch. I wasn't into silly convertibles, pools, or young lovers. Not me. I wanted to quit work and go back to college and try to become a writer. I applied to a graduate writing program near his town and was accepted with a full ride and tiny teaching stipend. There was one complication: it came with no health insurance.

We had never thought about marriage before. We'd been denied it so that when it became legal, it felt like an unnecessary afterthought. If we weren't allowed to participate in it back then when we were younger, then we didn't want any part of it when we were older. We had no need for a registry and gifts, but health insurance was vital to our lives. Very nonchalantly over the phone, he said to me, "well we can get married, and you can be on my insurance." Our marriage was transactional, but my love for him was anything but. Like he has always done in my mess of a life, Ric had a solution that came with a sense of ease. He always has a sense of ease.

During the early stages of the pandemic of 2020, while the world was afraid of Covid-19, I was exposed to a far deadlier virus. No one told me that rabies was so deadly, and that getting bit by a rabid animal was so dangerous and costly. It wasn't my first scare with a virus, nonetheless one of epidemic levels. I was in my early twenties during the 1990s, and like most sexually active gay men, had a very near encounter with HIV.

Just prior to the pandemic, when I thought my teaching and course load would keep me away from home for long periods of time, we decided to adopt a cat to keep our elderly dog company. We'd always had a menagerie of animals. At our height, we housed three dogs, two cats, two turtles, and a bunny. But after years of adoptions and deaths, we were down to one. Our dear sweet Alex was a yellow lab with a heart as big as could be. He was a social animal and missing his buddy cat that I'd named Brenda Walsh, who had passed that fall. Fearing that he would feel isolated, we decided to go to the local shelter and get a cat. This tiny beast rubbed up to Ric, climbed his back, and wrapped himself around his neck. I panicked and looked for any cat to choose me, but it was already over. Pets always love my husband a bit more than me. They sense my desperate need for attention. Next thing I knew, we filled out paperwork at the local shelter and adopted Jupiter (changed to Glen later that night).

During the pandemic winter months, a domesticity settled inside of me. I had moved only eight months prior. I knew no one, had no friends. I was a 47-year-old gay man starting grad school and living in a town surrounded by MAGA signs. Domestic life wore me into submission. I had to find the acceptance of this life, or it would rot me from the inside out thinking of the life I had back in Atlanta. I had signed up for a new life at a university, not an online life, one in an office attic where I pondered what to make for dinner.

Neither Ric nor I envisioned our first year of married life would be this way. While his life went virtually uninterrupted at work, mine was flipped on its head. He was sympathetic that I was no Betty Draper, but circumstances in the form of a virus was forcing the Betty Draper life on me. It was not the first time a virus had impacted our behavior. We'd lived through the onset of the AIDS crisis. That experience with an epidemic gave us a much-needed perspective to cope with this pandemic where people lost their minds over toilet paper and masks.

Right before the pandemic shut down the world, we'd started a remodel on the kitchen and removed the flowered wallpaper, terrible speckled vinyl flooring, and gutted the porous drop ceiling tiles. Deep in my sleep one night I felt a nibble, and weight, on my bare chest. I yelled at Glen and swatted what I thought was his squeaky bird toy off my naked chest. I heard white noise that I thought was from the TV. It wasn't.

I didn't see it at first. Glen was at the door sitting proudly upright. He trotted slowly to the middle of the room and nodded. I swear he nodded. I looked in the corner and there it was. A bat. Flapping with one wounded wing. Comically flapping as if it could escape. Then it dawned on me and I examined my chest. I woke Ric up and forced him to examine my chest. That is what I love about him: he takes care of things. And while he took care of things, I turned all the lights on in the bathroom and examined my chest hair in the mirror. I had started to gray and didn't even notice. I grabbed some tweezers and started plucking. When that proved laborious, I got the clippers and shaved my chest hairs. Then I proceeded to shave everywhere. Meanwhile, Ric got one of the many empty Amazon boxes and captured the injured bat and threw it out the back door.

Two days later I was in the same bathroom, a room that also was in a stalled Covid-19 renovation. I was examining body hair to see if other places had begun to gray. That bathroom had tube fluorescent lights that ran parallel to the mirror. They time traveled to my new life from 1976. They don't turn on immediately. Instead, they warm up. While warming up they have a white noise sound. But this day, the noise stayed after they warmed up. I tapped the light. I turned it off. I still heard the white noise. Glen was sitting on the bed. He nodded. I swear he nodded. I looked down and stepped on it with my bare foot. Another wing wounded bat. I was alone in the house and I could man up and deal with it or close the door and wait for my husband to get home to take care of it. Instead, I got my tennis racquet and another empty Amazon box, caught it, and threw that invader out the back door. I have great pride I did this removal naked.

The game commission agent showed up two days later responding to our call.

He advised me to get treatment before any symptoms present. He felt the bat most likely was rabid but would let us know. I called Ric and wondered if I should get the treatment. He wondered why I was even wondering. He was advised to get the treatment too since he'd been in contact with the bat saliva.

The word treatment is used lightly here. First they weigh you, and then determine how much rabies immune globulin to shoot in your ass. I needed two rounds. Ric needed three. I teased him about his weight. The globulin provides anti-bodies until the vaccine kicks in and you produce your own to fight the virus.

After the immunoglobulin treatment, I had to go back every seven days for three more shots of vaccine. The vaccine that is the same active ingredient that animals get. The same one that cost our cat, Glen, about fifty bucks. I began to panic about the money once I Googled "human rabies vaccine costs." When it was all totaled, it amounted to almost forty thousand dollars for both of us to get the vaccine. While marriage seemed an afterthought in our lives, I am thankful for it once those bills started rolling in and were covered by the insurance I had through our legal marriage.

It's funny that in my entire twenties and early thirties my mind thought a lot about a virus. If you were a sexually active gay man in the 1990s, HIV was a deep concern. Perhaps getting through those negative years gave me the coping mechanism to get through the Covid pandemic. While I watched people lose their minds over masks and bars closing, I settled in and hunkered down. I had a dog and a cat and bats flying about to keep me occupied. While the bill for the rabies vaccine awestruck me, I can only imagine the cost of other viruses over a lifetime.

The author with his husband.

Edward Jackson is a writer and educator whose prose has appeared in various literary outlets. He holds degrees in English and Education, including an MFA from Youngstown State University. He lives in the Midwest with his husband and a menagerie of pets. Reel Around the Fountain *is his debut novel.*

How Chat Rooms Helped Me Figure Out I'm Trans

By Dev Jannerson

Around 2013 I noticed a new thought gnawing at my mind. No, I thought, it's not possible. I thought about all the reasons it couldn't be true, flipping through photographic evidence from political rallies to concerts to dresses. I'm a girl. Everyone knows it.

I hopped into chat rooms—yes, chat rooms still existed—as a trans guy named Clive. I dreamed up a whole character for him. I assumed this impulse stemmed from my PTSD and was simply a fantasy about being someone else. Clive was confident and athletic and had a Gothic, rugged Adam Lambert aesthetic.

He didn't stay in the chat room. I was planning for the future for the first time, and it was easier to imagine myself as an old man than an old woman, as a dad than a mom. I felt like a charlatan in groups of women, even when they were all queer. I was surprised every time I saw myself in the mirror, and had been for as long as I could remember. I'd once argued with transphobic people; now, even being near them overwhelmed me with panic. I stopped dressing high-femme, because it used to feel like I gained power with every compliment, but now it felt icky. I dreamed of being two different people: an embattled woman the world had already proven they'd kind of accept and a flamboyant man whom they might not. He would stay hidden, just to be safe.

In early 2017, I asked my fiancée if she was sure she wanted to marry me—even if my depression got scary again, even if I turned out to be a guy. She did. I continued to talk to her about my feelings, but not to anyone else, save the occasional therapist. She started calling me a boy in private. It felt wonderful.

I anonymously posted on Reddit. They told me to meet some other trans people, read Stone Butch Blues. They were nice, but I bristled. I read Stone Butch Blues fifteen years ago, thank you very much! I've had trans friends since George W.! I once drunk-texted Kate Bornstein! I had written a novel about growing up lesbian.

If this were a real thing, I thought, wouldn't it have come up then? Surely it was too late.

In 2018, Daniel Lavery told Autostraddle: "It turns out I'm trans." Every word he spoke after that sounded like my interior monologue, only confident.

More than a decade after it happened, I thought about the fact that it took me until college to start publicly dating women. A sense of My life cannot possibly fit anything else haunted me. I'd been the Sick Kid by the time I turned ten, the one everyone felt entitled to follow around asking invasive questions and harassing about their diet. I safely rebelled by defending my gay friends, supporting marriage equality. I dated boys. For some reason, the ones I really liked were queer, too. I wasn't happy, but I read the same magazines as everyone else, and straight women didn't seem happy either.

I tried not to come out, until I could not try anymore. I had to be pro-queer for the sake of everyone around me before I could extend that same understanding to myself. Around 2015, I saw that I was on a similar trajectory with gender. Again, I resisted.

Every once in a while, when I was thinking about my own gender but wasn't thinking about other people, the voice would pop up more clearly: I'm trans. It felt like a bucket of cold water every single time. My idea of Clive was changing. He looked and seemed more like ... me. Still, I bargained, trying to satisfy it with androgyny and role playing. My life is too much already. I could be trans ... if I were someone else. If I had grown up with a functional family. If I hadn't been raised in a "Focus on the Family" environment. If I were younger, say, Gen Z. If I were Daniel Lavery.

As for my insistence that it was already too late, when would I have done it, exactly? When I wasn't even living in a safe place? When my PTSD first manifested after Katrina? When I moved across the country (any of the times)? When I struggled to make enough money to survive? When I lived for my next article, my next award, my next book?

In my teens and twenties, I reveled in the ways clothes and makeup and jewelry allowed me to express myself. It felt like drag, but in a fun way. Was my identity as a woman based in that same need to feel as normal as possible? After all, everyone told me I was a girl. If I couldn't recognize myself, did I want to play the part I'd been given as well as I could? Maybe, but it didn't make women's groups any less valuable, and it didn't make dealing with sexism any easier. I understood myself to be a girl, and then a woman.

I think that I was one, or close enough. But I'm not now. And I'm not Clive either. I'm something else, someone else. I hope you'll like him. Either way, Dev isn't staying hidden.

The author and wife Kelsey at their wedding in June 2017. [Photo: Samantha Abney]

Dev Jannerson is an award-winning author of novels, short stories, and essays for teens and adults. Jannerson is a 2025 Lambda Literary Fellow, a two-time Tin House graduate, and a Pushcart and Best of the Net nominee. He is represented by Lee O'Brien of Looking Glass Literary & Media and lives in New Orleans with a cat named Goat.

Editor's Note: A different version of this article was previously published on Medium.com.

Notes on Queerness in Quarantine

By Francesca Capossela

THE KINSEY SCALE charts queerness in thick, stacked blocks along an x-axis, skyscrapers of identity. The scale ranges from zero, for completely heterosexual, to six, for completely homosexual, with everything else in between. But my sexuality felt like a wave or a season, something closer to the earth and harder to measure. It wasn't one half of every second. It was seasonal affective disorder; allergies every spring. The need to swim during the warm months. It shifted with the tide, with the movements of the planets and the moon. And every time I thought I knew myself, I changed.

At different points in my life, I have worn my hair cropped close to my head and long, down my back. I've called myself Francesco and Francesca, Ella and Beck. I've worn boxers and thongs, baseball caps and crop tops, bikinis and swimming trunks. Everywhere I go, I have belonged and not belonged. Largely, I have been okay with this discordance; I have accepted it.

But, during the height of the COVID-19 pandemic, living with my then-boyfriend, I began to feel that I had lost something, like a favorite sweater forgotten on some subway train. I had felt estranged from my queerness before, by default of being in a straight relationship, but I had always been able to feel secure within queer spaces. Without those spaces, I was lost.

I missed the parts of me that I no longer seemed to have access to, the self I could only be around other queer people. I missed June in New York City, that fleeting sense of belonging, like Gretel finding the breadcrumbs she left for herself, following them home. I missed the way being with people like me made me feel bulletproof and ravenous. The smell of garbage, the suck of an afternoon cocktail, the buzz of last night's hangover with music playing: You can dance, you can jive.

Francesca at a wedding around nine years old.

In separating us from each other, isolation robbed us of ourselves. The way we are allowed to be only when we travel in packs or pairs, the selves we need help digging out, unburying. It is not the first disease to whittle away at our pride, to make us wonder how we can face the world, us being who we are, the world being how the world is. Of course, we needed isolation. We needed it to keep us, and each other, safe. And, maybe, we needed it in another way. Maybe we needed it because it forced us to look deeper at ourselves. At the lives we were leading and the communities we depended on. And just as important, who we are when we are alone.

When my boyfriend and I broke up, it wasn't because he was a man. Or, it wasn't only. It was because, after five years, we had become different versions of ourselves, yearning to explore our own interests and desires, and we found that these no longer overlapped like they once had.

It was heartbreak, of course. But, at the same time, it seemed we had learned to be more ourselves. We had learned it, in many ways, from each other, and from the strange year we'd spent alone together.

He had helped to show me who I was. Now, I needed to follow the breadcrumbs back home.

When NYC lifted stay at home orders in 2021, I went to Henrietta Hudson, one of the only still-standing lesbian bars in the city. Someone I'd just met had called Henrietta ahead of time, and asked: "Can you take twenty dykes right now?"

We sat at a long table, and I drank a beer too fast, nervous. I wondered why I was even there, in a group of strangers who all knew each other. I was with members of the Dyke March planning committee, which I'd joined late; it was already June, and these people had been working together since February or March. I'd joined in an attempt at rediscovering community.

But, sitting there, I felt like an intruder.

"Honey," an older dyke to my right said. "Could you pass me the water?"

The endearment in her rough voice. Her certainty, despite not knowing me, that I was like her. Her commitment to loving me, no matter who I was, because of who I was.

The waiter took our drink orders. She had a pair of scissors tattooed on her hand. Someone complimented it, and she told us how a woman had asked her if she was a hairdresser.

We all laughed. And, suddenly, I could feel the small thread between us: it was a language we all spoke, a secret we'd all kept as children. I relaxed and turned to the people beside me, and got to talking.

I met many of the people I now call my best friends that spring, as we sat in meetings planning the Dyke March. I had sought out this community, inorganic and planned, but I was surprised by the ways it embraced me. I was surprised by the people I met who made me feel at home, like I was family. The things we did, and discussed, were trivial: who hooked up with whom, who had drama with their ex, what feuds erupted that week. We glanced up at passersby and guessed if they were queer. We checked out the same girls. But there was more to it than that, something underneath. Months into our friendship, a friend of mine realized she had no idea what one of our best friends did for work. In a way, it was damning. Why did we never talk about our nine-to-five lives, our career goals? But in another way, it was what made us special: when we were together, we lived in our own world, a world that revolved around queerness. When we left each other, we returned to the colorless world of presumed heterosexuality and corporate America, a fraction of ourselves missing.

It was when I was with straight people that I most realized who I was. When they talked about their first kisses and first times. When they talked about their parents, about introducing their boyfriends. When they sat in a bar and did not wonder how they were being read, if they were being clocked. It was not that I was living in fear in Manhattan in 2021. But some part of me was always thinking about who I was. And when I was not with people like me, that awareness was not shared. That part of me, they could not understand.

And then there was the way we could talk about shame. The way it hung behind so many of our conversations. The way I understood when my best friend—who would later become my girlfriend, and even later, my wife— told me that her parents knew but also didn't know she was gay. How she could feel what I'd felt the first time I heard the word queer as a slur, coming out of the mouth of someone I loved. To each other, we did not have to explain these things. And, being with her, the world around me quieted.

Somewhere inside me, I knew I had been dreaming of her all my life.

In 2021, the Dyke March took all four lanes of Fifth Avenue for the first time since 1997.

And I was running alongside the beast of the parade, the body of the protest. I stopped at the faces I knew, faces I loved. The people who had planned this, who had led me through the process, who had made me feel welcome. I wondered if, maybe once upon a time, they too had been young and afraid, and maybe, sometimes, they still were. I stopped and grinned at them, and they grinned back, and it was greater than a kiss, that feeling.

There was still so much I did not know. It would be months before I first called myself a lesbian. Years before I married my wife. But I was moving towards who I was becoming: I was running and my heart was racing, and my fist was closed around something hidden in the sand, a memory as old as Patroclus, as old as Sappho: we do not exist in isolation. We are most ourselves when we find each other.

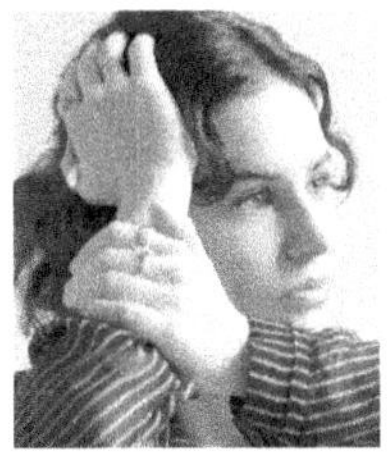

Francesca grew up in Brooklyn and holds a Master's from Trinity College Dublin. Her debut novel, Trouble the Living, *came out in 2024. She lives with her wife and dog.*

The Cost of
Bottom Surgery

By Emmitt Barnes

AMONG SOME COMMUNITIES of trans men, the sentiment that getting phalloplasty is an impossibility is fairly common. Between the high risk for physical complications and financial burden, it's no wonder many guys who want bottom surgery don't get it. After getting phalloplasty myself and dealing with the medical and financial complications, I found the financial aspect of the surgery more difficult than the physical. The only way I could afford this surgery was by limiting my income so that my surgeries were covered by Medi-Cal. It's kept me from marrying my partner, progressing in my career, and building savings. These sacrifices are amplified by the physical journey of now having a working penis. You'd think after so much sacrifice and hardship I wouldn't recommend this surgery to those who want it, but you'd be wrong.

For those uninitiated, phalloplasty is the kind of bottom surgery which aims to give the patient a life size, workable, and realistic penis. It takes a large square of flesh, often from the forearm or thigh, and grafts it into a tube shape over the natal genitalia, where a plastic surgeon fashions it into the likeness of a penis. A phalloplasty can be made to enable standing to urinate, penetrative sex, and other similar functions.

If one wants to stand to pee, then the entire urethra gets lengthened, and that's where a majority of the complications lie. If someone wants to have sex without the aid of external prosthetics, implants are placed inside the new organ. Each 'feature' requires an extra surgical step, and with every step comes the possibility of complications, some of which are treated with simple antibiotics and patience, while others require surgical intervention.

I knew I was prone to complications from my experience with top surgery, but I wanted a penis that could do everything a cis penis could do. I jumped in with both feet. I had to get electrolysis hair removal on my arm for over a year before surgery, going in weekly for two to three hours to a nice lady who would take a hot needle to every follicle on my arm. This was so that I wouldn't grow hair in my new urethra and so that my new dick wouldn't come out looking like a hairy caterpillar.

After electrolysis, I went to the surgeons. Both a urologist and a plastic surgeon were a part of my team, so I had to drive out to meet with both teams several times for various consultations and check-ups. Early on I realized that if I had a nine-to-five job I would have lost it before I ever had a chance to have surgery. My surgical team was two and a half hours away from my home, and my trans affirming primary care was an hour away. My electrolysis lady was an hour away, and none were in the same direction. I was averaging one day a week that I would have to take off work to get surgery rolling. When I figured out a rhythm to seeing my electrolysis lady after work, I was able to get a job that claimed to be amenable to my sporadic attendance. Then, during the summer of 2024, I got the surgery.

I had more complications than what is statistically likely for this surgery (Radial Forearm Flap graft urethroplasty can expect 53.3% likelihood of complications according to one study). I wasn't surprised when I had a hole that urine leaks from, called a fistula, but having seven was virtually unheard of. After three different surgeries, they all healed. Then came the strictures, which made it so I couldn't urinate at all. I had surgery for that this week, and since this was an urgent issue I had to drop everything to get it fixed.

When I started having strictures my flexible job could no longer accommodate my frequent absences, and I had to go back to temp work, which was a significant pay cut. When I look back on my phalloplasty experience, all I can think is: "how the hell does anyone afford this?" Electrolysis was covered by my insurance, but for many trans men it isn't. The average session of electrolysis costs $75 dollars an hour, sometimes more. This can add up to thousands of dollars, and that's before the cost of surgery even enters the picture. Every single surgery I had was necessary to repair complications, but if I had to pay even the copays for all of them I would be in serious financial trouble.

For comparison, I talked to a guy who got the same kind of phalloplasty as me from the same surgical team who had insurance. His insurance did not pay for electrolysis, he paid $3,600 dollars for that. After the initial surgery, a revision, and an emergency hospital stay he owes $8,500 to the hospital. He is lucky enough to live in the same city as his surgeon, so he didn't have to pay for a place to stay while he recovered or gas to travel extensively. Many trans men have to temporarily relocate to have this surgery due to how few surgeons perform it, adding to the already daunting costs. According to a study from the National Library of Medicine that was published in 2022 "the median total cost was $148,540" out of pocket for phalloplasty without insurance in the United States. If you're an American reading this you might be jaded hearing the obscene cost for medical procedures, but to many trans men, these costs are why they don't pursue gender affirming surgery.

I think the financial aspect of phalloplasty is one of the biggest barriers. I see on the online message boards people living like monks, saving every penny and living in questionable situations so that they can save up for phalloplasty. Without insurance, many save thousands of dollars to prepare for surgery, for housing needed to be close to surgeons during recovery, and additional medical supplies like bandages. I know I can't be the only person who lost income and job opportunities due to the medical emergencies that come with phalloplasty.

While it's true that this is a high risk versus reward procedure, the financial implications attached to the physical complications compound the existing strains the preparation and initial surgery put on one's finances. If we are to make this an accessible surgery, the financial barriers must be lifted. A more socialized healthcare would alleviate the financial stress and would be a great help to the trans male community. Having the state's help kept me from truly losing all financial stability; others deserve the same support.

Emmitt Barnes is an author and artist based in San Bernardino, California. His work has been published in Backstory Journal, Skateism *magazine,* Croak, *and the* Shishir Poetry Collection.

Wanting

An Italian-American traveler in Buenos Aires becomes a stand-in for a deceased boyfriend. A Nigerian man is lured via Grindr into a "kito" ambush. A Moroccan man finds the community in Vietnam that he could not find at home. The stories in this chapter interrogate the luxury of exploration, the shame and beauty of discovery, approaching questions about desire, lack, and how we investigate our curiosities.

Surviving a Kito Experience

By Osadolor Edokpayi

THERE ARE MEMORIES you wish you could lock away, bury deep within the recesses of your mind, never to be revisited. For me, this is one of them. But as I sit here sharing my story, I do so with the hope that it sheds light on a harrowing reality many have faced and continue to face in Nigeria. This is what it means to be "kitoed," and how I survived.

It was December 2021, two days after Christmas. I had traveled from Enugu, where I worked, to spend the holidays with my family in Lagos. It had been a year since I last saw them, and I was determined to make the most of my two week holiday. I wanted this Christmas to be one to remember.

My first morning there, as the warmth of the Lagos sun crept through the windows, I was lazing in bed when my phone buzzed. A message appeared from someone I'd been chatting with on Grindr for a couple of weeks. "Are you free?" he asked. His name was familiar, and we'd shared lighthearted conversations about movies, music, and family. Nothing overtly flirtatious or sexual. Just casual banter.

"Yes, I am," I replied.

"Can you please come around? I'm preparing noodles. My folks went to church." It seemed harmless. My mind, innocent and unsuspecting, didn't sense any red flags. It was just a friendly visit.

"Alright, I'll come around," I agreed. After sleeping in a bit longer, I freshened up, dressed, and texted him to let him know I was on my way.

He sent me directions, and soon I was on the move. At the bus stop near his place, he arrived on a motorbike to pick me up.

"Hop on," he said, gesturing for me to sit between him and the bike man. Alarm bells went off in my head. I had heard too many stories of kidnappings that began just like this. I politely refused and insisted he sit in the middle while I sit at the back. Reluctantly, he agreed.

As we rode, I began to notice something strange. People were watching us, really watching us. Their stares. Their stares felt invasive, almost accusatory. A chill ran down my spine, but I brushed it off. Then, the bike veered off into a bushy, run-down area. Five men stood ahead, waiting. My heart sank. I knew was in trouble.

I jumped off the bike in a desperate attempt to flee, but didn't get far. They cornered me, dragging me back like a helpless animal. Their fists rained down on me. Punches, kicks, slaps. I screamed for help, but passersby turned a blind eye, pretending not to see. My cries went unanswered.

They took me deeper into an isolated area. There, they stripped me of everything—my chain, my sandals, my bracelet, even my clothes. All I had left were my briefs. They laughed as they burned me with cigarettes, a twisted form of amusement. Then one of them, the guy l trusted and had originally come to see, walked up to me.

"Look, if you cooperate, we no go kill you. You a gentle boy," he said, as if his words were supposed to comfort me. Then, he demanded my ATM card and PIN. With no choice, I gave it to him. Two of them left to withdraw all my money while the others continued to beat me senseless.

The man who initially lured me there started talking about his hatred for queer people. He told me his younger brother had been raped by ten men, and now he saw himself as some sort of vigilante. His reasoning was warped, his justification pathetic. What did his brother's tragedy have to do with me? I was tired. Exhausted from the weight of their fists. Desperately wishing it was all a bad dream.

Osadolor is a creative storyteller who believes the African queer narrative isn't told enough in mainstream media. According to him, "Not all African queer stories have sad endings. We aren't focused enough on the beautiful stories." He also writes in other niches, such as business and lifestyle.

My Trick List:
A Personal
Names Project

By Randolph Tibbits

Rereading tennessee williams's *Memoirs* recently, I came across this line: "But then life is full of transient loves when you are young."

His poignantly poetic line sent me searching for reminders of my own transient loves of youth, which is how I rediscovered my list, long forgotten, written in pencil on tablet paper, smudged and yellowing for dramatic effect. I don't remember when I compiled the list. 1985? 1990? It's hard to be sure now.

Though I didn't put a title on it then, I will now: "My Trick List." There they are, the 123 men I've had sex with. There's no use denying it: many were one-night stands. Some were repeats over days or weeks. Some were periodic fuckbuddies over years. Three or four were even lovers, though "lover" sounds so dated now, in the age of husbands.

One hundred and twenty-three: not very many, maybe, compared to sexual super-gays like Samuel Steward, aka Phil Andros, who meticulously noted on index cards details about thousands of his own tricks over a lifetime—including names like Rudolph Valentino and Rock Hudson. In defense of my own gay prowess, I'll note that mine all happened in a few short years in the 1970s, before I met the man who is now my husband. His name is the last one on my list.

Not all 123 are "names," exactly—more like identifiers in many cases, because sometimes I forgot the names, or never knew them. Drugs, sex, and discotheques don't make for great name recall. For example, Number 6 is "American in Paris" and Number 73 is "Largest Personality (in Chicago)."

How I wish I could remember more about Number 1: "Flyboy in Cotton Field." There was an Air Force base in the town where I grew up, and I do remember how good he looked, standing at attention in uniform, and out of it. It's probably best that I don't remember more about Number 47, "Awful," or Number 82, "The One I Walked Out On." I'm sure they would both agree that it's best to admit your mistakes early and just get out.

I seem to have had my international period: "Brazilian in New Haven"; "Hot Italian"; "Key West Portuguese." And my religious phase: "X-Mormon"; "Franciscan Brother"; "MCC Minister."

"Callipygous redhead in K.C." sure takes me back. "San Francisco, Into Bondage" and "Abuse from NC" make me a little queasy now, and "FFA, Fist Full of ..." makes me a little faint. "Hard As Two Rocks, St. Louis" is unforgettable, but "Cincinnati Airline Pilot" is only the vaguest memory. He was not a flight to remember.

"First True Love" I remember vividly, his corn-silk hair, his lean chest, his blue eyes—cutting, steel-blue eyes as it turned out—and the memory brings a wistful tear to my own eye even now.

Since this is the information age, I decided to see what I could find out about some of those who are actual names on my list, rather than just identifiers.

I didn't find "First True Love," but I did find "Rush, in New York"—such a sweet, hot guy—though he lit my first cigarette for me, so I really shouldn't be so indulgent toward him. He went back to his Mississippi home to die in 1983, the cause not much doubt. And I located "Gary Who Loved Sex"—at least a memory of him in a church bulletin from later on. He moved to San Francisco at exactly the wrong time for a man so into having other men so into him.

I had no idea that "John the Professor," now also gone, was so much older than I, or that he had a wife. "Med Student Karl" is still with us, having practiced medicine in a Midwestern state for forty years. "Jason the gorgeous" I found in another memoir via Google Books—Young Man From the Provinces: A Gay Life Before Stonewall, by Alan Helms, a handsome, glamorous "golden boy" of 1950s Gay New York, who later transformed himself into an English professor. He's my one degree of separation from the gay, beautiful, and famous of another age.

I found a few more, but not many. It was long ago, and many didn't make it to the Internet age.

When I wrote my list it seemed like life was winding down—certainly youth was—and that I might not have much time left. I figured I'd better write things down fast before my memory faded. Now, thirty-plus years later, life is still winding down, but I can still pretty much remember. As it turned out, I'm one of those lucky enough to get old, but certainly there can't be much time left now.

For many of my 123, there's no time left at all, but perhaps it means something that I remember them, even if only as "Hair Weave on Westminster" or "Banker and Urologist" (oops, two for one that time—make that 124). Maybe some of the ones who are still around remember me too. Maybe they've even written me down. That would be "Insecure, buns not of steel, drank too much, but not absolutely awful" (except probably for one or two), or however they identified me on their list. I admit I'd sort of like to know.

I guess I could ask my husband how he listed me after that first night way back when. But maybe I won't. After forty years together, I'll just assume I rated at least okay with him.

The author in Saint Louis, Missouri, 1972.

Randolph Tibbits is an old grey gay guy who lives in Houston, Texas, with his husband of 45 years. He's old enough to know better, but still young enough not to let that stop him—sometimes. He writes "Saint Louis Blues—Gay Days and Nights in the 1970s" and other things on Substack.

The Attendant

By Alessandro Ghidini

"**So, where are you from?**"

The question from the young man at the front desk was a typical icebreaker. Mark and I were trying to bide our time until dinner on the last evening of our vacation in Buenos Aires. Mark had chosen to have a massage, while I opted to lounge in the lobby by the front desk, where the handsome attendant was handing out towels and serving drinks. The lighting was diffuse and relaxing. The guy looked to be in his early twenties. Under the arches of thick black eyebrows, his deep, black velvety eyes had a magnetic pull, and the dimples on his cheeks when he smiled were irresistible.

"I am from Italy," I said.

My answer was partly true. Though I had been born in Italy, I'd lived most of my life in the U.S. But, what with the desaparacidos by the U.S.-backed Argentinian military regime in the '70s, I opted for safety.

"That's great!" he replied. "I am studying Italian. Perhaps you could help me with my homework."

I had noticed that in between clients he was reading and writing. Sure, I would be delighted to help. We switched from English to Italian. I told him I was living in the U.S. He had never visited the U.S., but it was one of his dreams. He wanted to quit this job and study to become a flight attendant; hence his interest in foreign languages. I could think of several other languages more practical than Italian for work in the travel industry.

"I started studying Italian for my boyfriend," he told me. "He was Argentinian, but his family was from Italy and they spoke some Italian at home."

So, there was some history here. He used the past tense, but his words still showed affection for this boyfriend. Was he on the rebound from being dumped? I was curious but did not probe beyond what he was willing to share.

"How did you like Buenos Aires?" he asked.

Of course I loved it. I recounted our adventures at the usual tourist places, including the tomb of Evita Perón in the cemetery of Recoleta, near our hotel. Somehow going through a cemetery seemed perfect for the season. We had left the U.S. with trees starting to sprout new leaves, while in Argentina the plane trees lining the avenues had already started to shed their leaves. Finally Mark reappeared. "I had a great massage, do you want to have one too?"

"No," I answered. "I think I'll pass. Do you want to keep looking around the place?"

Mark noticed the guy behind the desk, drew his own conclusions, and left to spend some more time sniffing around.

We resumed our banter as if it had never been interrupted. No, he had not broken up with his boyfriend, who had been the love of his life. After living together for a few years, he had died of an acute leukemia in his mid-thirties three months earlier. The death had made him reconsider many things, including whether to continue with this job, which his boyfriend had always hated. Work in the airline industry sounded like a great opportunity for new beginnings and adventures, and for putting the sadness of the last months behind. But, he confided, it would not be easy in a country cursed with inflation and the resulting turmoil. All young people were desperate to find jobs or move abroad.

Speaking in Italian gave us a sense of complicity. Our conversation was periodically interrupted by clients who needed a new towel or drinks or, I was certain, to flirt with the handsome attendant. He responded courteously and gave them a smile before returning to my corner of the desk. What was going on here? Was he really only interested in practicing Italian? Was he hoping to find a sugar daddy to sponsor his studies? Could he be attracted physically? Despite keeping myself in good shape, I was undeniably in my late forites. Mark reappeared, satisfied after a shower, and we were both ready to go. On the way out, the attendant smiled at me one last time and discreetly handed me a piece of paper with his phone number.

"I would like to see you again," he said.

"My flight is tomorrow afternoon."

"Let's have a coffee in the morning?" he offered.

We agreed to meet at 11 o'clock the next day at a café in his neighborhood, Palermo.

I arrived at the coffee shop early. From my table I could keep an eye on the entrance. Would he really come? But there he was. People turned around to look at his beaming face. We drank a coffee, but he seemed to be in a hurry; I wondered whether he had only come out of politeness.

"Would you like to come to my apartment?" he asked "It's nearby, and we can walk there."

The invitation caught me by surprise, but I answered: "Of course"

His apartment was modest but clean and bright. He put on some music while I was looking around. On a low table were some framed photographs, among them one of a handsome young man smiling at the camera, oddly familiar.

"Who is this one?" I asked.

"My boyfriend."

I looked more closely, and then I suddenly realized it: the guy looked like me when I was my thirties. The resemblance was uncanny. Finally it all made sense, but before I could say anything, his hands and his lips were on me, hugging, kissing, pulling my clothes off with fury and passion, dragging me to his bed while talking in a fast and plaintive Argentinian Spanish. I could not make out what he was saying, but it didn't matter: he was not talking to me.

I cried in the taxi on the way back to the hotel, and I cried more on the flight back home.

Though I never went back to Buenos Aires, that was not the last time that I would see him. But that's a story for another time.

Alessandro Ghidini is a physician and professor at a medical
school. He is passionate about piano playing and ballroom dancing.
He loves animals and currently has 3 dogs and 10 cats.

A Neon Rainbow in a Vietnamese Alleyway

By Akram Herrak

I DON'T KNOW WHAT I expected from a gay bar—the closest I've ever gotten to being in one was when I went to a drag show in Beirut, Lebanon, and still, the place was filled with large groups of friends and a few straight couples, and I suspected the only people there who were queer were the performers themselves. Two and a half years later, I again found myself far from home, and it is only this distance that can remind me that people don't have to live in the shadows if they don't want to.

Vietnam proved to be a wonderful place of chaos and serenity, where you could walk the streets of Hanoi in the midst of a million scooters swaying around you, wondering how you've not been hit yet, and then ride one yourself for a few hours and end up in the middle of nowhere, the most beautiful 'nowhere' you've ever seen.

Five hundred miles south of the capital is the ancient town of Hoi An: a gem, a little hidden gem as an old French guy described it to me. And he was half right. A gem it really was, lined with historic buildings coated in sunflower yellow with lanterns dangling in-between and a river that cuts through the entirety of the town, always filled with little boats carrying tourists who joyfully light candles and set them down the river. But it was anything but hidden. During peak hours, you could hardly walk through all the crowds, and it didn't matter if it was a Tuesday or a Saturday, people were always there.

After a little while in Hoi An, I was fortunate enough to meet a Vietnamese girl who grew up in America and returned to reconnect with her roots, and she offered to show me around. After spending a few hours together, we were both comfortable enough to tell each other that we were both bisexual. In our accepting atmosphere, which was a complete novelty to me as I never disclosed my sexuality back home, she mentioned that a new gay bar had just opened in town and she asked if I wanted to go there. Very gladly, I said yes.

At 10 that night, I rode my bicycle out of the touristy old town into a hidden street where I saw a neon sign glowing in the colors of the rainbow. I parked and went in. The place was full but quiet, men sat around in groups around tables or at the bar and chatted over drinks. I saw my friend sitting with four guys and she waved to me. Very timidly, I said hi and introduced myself to the two Australian men, one in his thirties and one in his sixties, the American guy in his thirties, and the Filipino young man who was the most energetic. My friend and I exchanged looks and I saw worry in her eyes. She suspected I might be out of my element, and she was right. I turned to the bartender and ordered a gin and tonic. I heard a faint French accent when he spoke and said merci when he gave me the drink. With a big smile, he asked me if I was French, and I said no, I'm Moroccan. We exchanged a few words about life in Vietnam before he had to go back to work. I asked him for an ashtray, and he handed me one completely in black with a big cock erected in the middle of it. I sipped on my drink and smoked my cigarette and dropped the ash on the tip of the ashtray's cock.

My friend suggested we all move to a couch, so we followed her. Once we sat down, the old Australian man turned to me and asked me if I wanted a cigarette. He then pulled out a pack of Marlboro Gold with two cigarettes left. Out of politeness, I said, "You only have two left," and he said, "It's okay, I just bought another pack." And after a small pause, he looked at me and said, "I also have another pack here," while grabbing his cock and laughing.

We smoked our cigarettes in quiet afterward. He thought he made a move too quickly and I could see he was trying to fix it, but I was just amused. I had no interest in meeting anyone, I was only there to observe and listen. A couple of minutes later, he turned to me and said, "We all have that one man in our lives, don't we? The one we know would be perfect for us but for some reason it never works out. Who's that for you?" And I thought about it for a minute but could not think of anyone, so I said, "I have yet to meet him."

He wanted to tell me about his. They met in college and decided to drop out and join the military together. He spoke to me of their love in the closet, hidden away from a society that would've sent them both to jail. He spoke of him as Baldwin speaks of Giovanni. Abruptly, his story cut to twenty years later and his unnamed lover is married with a kid. It had been twenty years since they last spoke, and they randomly stumbled upon each other online and decided to catch up. With a sad smile, he told me about how great of a woman his wife is, and how much fun he had hiking with his kid and getting to know him as one of his dad's old military buddies. Before they said goodbye again, his old lover turned to him completely unprovoked and said, "You know I can never leave my wife."

He spoke to me about how much progress he had made in those twenty years and how he learned to let go of the man he thought was perfect for him, and how much damage that single sentence inflicted. Four years later, he was with me in a gay bar in Vietnam getting ready to see him again in a month, and as he told me how they're just good friends now and nothing more, I saw the battle in his head raging through his escaped excuses as he justified himself passionately for something I perfectly understood.

I don't know what I expected from a gay bar, but I'm happy with what I got. I saw love, I saw humanity in its most beautiful form, feeling down to the depths of its heart, and I saw cute guys flirting with each other all night. May y(our) love be easier. ▨

Akram is a writer focusing on film, literature, culture, and travel. His work has appeared in Reader's Digest, Thrillist, The Gay & Lesbian Review, *and others. He is the vocalist for death metal band Surged Fate, an amateur photographer, and a competitive chess player. You can read more from Akram and follow his substack https://akramherrak.substack.com.*

How It All Changed

By Bob Angell

At the LGBT march on Washington on April 25, 1993, Ben and I walked with our friends south on Ninth Street to the National Mall. We spread out picnic blankets half-way between the U.S. Capital and the Washington Monument, joining what would become over one million protestors. I'd been a reluctant witness to much of the evolution of gay rights. I'd seen and experienced things, good and bad. After decades of baby-steps, I was finally out everywhere except at work and was living a comfortable status quo. Despite the energy of the crowd, I felt sad and ashamed, a failure for still being in the closet at work.

I'd spent the last eleven years constructing a careful out life within the constraints I'd been given. The price of being a sheltered, private-school kid in the 1970s was that you trusted and believed the uniform societal norms that insulated you from the larger world. Homophobia was rampant and encouraged. Despite crushes on boys, the occasional girlfriend kept me 'safe' and on-track. I had a script to live. At Duke University, I joined a fraternity instead of exploring what it meant to be gay, in part because the new Gay and Lesbian Union office door was never open. My fraternity brothers knew I was a physics major and granted me occasional eccentricities.

After graduation in 1980, I landed a job at Westinghouse Defense and Electronic Systems Center during the worst job market since the Great

Depression. I worked in integrated circuit fabrication, which required a security clearance. Like my fraternity, the security clearance world forbade granting membership to homosexuals. And in my line of work, if you didn't have a clearance, you didn't have a job. I felt lucky, then guilty the following year when I stopped lying to myself and realized I had no choice: I was gay. However, in a southern family you learn at a young age to live with guilt and a conflicting self-images, so I had a leg up.

Flying to and from Silicon Valley for work allowed me to get back in touch with an old friend who had moved to Milwaukee. Lisa and I had been in ninth and tenth grades together in Maryland. We'd briefly dated before her family moved; I took her to her senior prom, during which she came out to me. That was why we got along so well. We both vanished into college and finally reconnected during layover weekends as I flew between the coasts. In the fall of 1981, she and her lover moved to Maryland and we rented a house together. I had community and a support group.

I came out to my parents expecting to be disowned and was surprised that they didn't kick me out of the family. By then I was a fully-fledged and self-sufficient adult. Soon after, in May 1982, Gay-Related Immune Deficiency—what AIDS was initially called—crashed the party, just as I was getting comfortable. It terrified me and I withdrew. I went from DC Pride parades in '81 and '82 to the AIDS Candlelight Vigil in 1983.

Getting healthy and looking healthy was important. I'd always been a runner and wanted to run a marathon when I turned thirty, so I quit smoking on my 29th birthday and started training for the Marine Corps Marathon. I got hooked and became a triathlete. Training gave me the perfect excuse not to socialize with coworkers and not to go to bars. I joined the gay swim team, DC/AC, and we volunteered to stay up all night guarding the AIDS Quilt in October 1987, the eve of another LGBT protest march.

In the nervous darkness, we walked the perimeter of the oval-shaped Ellipse in pairs, Reagan's White House guarded and uncaring in the background. The hand-made memorial panels for AIDS victims, folded under protective waterproof tarps, formed dark mounds in a precise grid covering the entire park. There were midnight threats, shivers, walky-talkies, and lots of strong coffee. In the crisp morning light, other volunteers came and unfolded the vibrant panels in reverent silence as a new day dawned.

The next October, I met Ben in a popular video bar in DC called Badlands. I saw him across the sea of mingling men and wished I had the guts to go say hello. Ben's friend noticed and shoved us together. "This guy's been watching you all night," his friend said. "Put him out of his misery."

Ben and I couldn't stop talking that night. Two years later we were living together. My coworkers thought I had a new roommate, but the secretaries knew better. "Ben is on line three," they said, and I could hear smiles in their voice.

My bosses started telling me stories about how their wives had gay hairdressers or how they took dancing lessons from a limp-wristed instructor on the weekends. The nice ones were making an attempt to be friendly, however cryptic or obtuse. Others were overtly hostile. I remained politely uncomfortable and semi-invisible. The government still forbade granting security clearances to homosexuals. I didn't have the guts to push anything, so I soldiered on and wondered about friendlier workplaces. Corporations were starting to market to gay people. Even better, tech companies were considering domestic partner benefits as a tool to lure or retain talent. I hoped that tolerance might be giving way to acceptance in places.

Then, on March 6, 1993, a personal setback: my mother married my stepfather. She told me she was afraid to tell him I was gay for fear he'd back out. I'd been with my partner for five years at that point, and out to my mother for eleven years. Ben was not invited to the wedding. To make sure I went, she put me in the ceremony. I was miserable, but I held it together until they cut the cake, and then I said my goodbyes. My new Irish-Catholic stepsiblings asked why I was leaving. After all, we'd had fun times together over the past year and this was a time to celebrate. I told them, "I'm going home to Ben, my partner. He wasn't invited."

To their credit, my five stepsiblings brought their spouses and kids down to our home in Greenbelt to apologize and welcome Ben into the new family. (Our parents weren't invited.) I realized I couldn't change my side of the family, but the new side could outnumber them. I was finally out to everyone, except at work.

Back at the National Mall the organizers set up giant screens called jumbotrons around the perimeter so everyone could see the staged events. Melissa Etheridge, RuPaul, and Madonna headlined. All around us, people came closer, and not only in proximity but in spirit, comradery, and purpose. We were there to demand rights, to get funding for AIDS research, and to remind Bill Clinton of his campaign promises. We were there to have fun and be together and be visible to the entire country.

We stripped off our tee-shirts, danced together in the sunlight, drank from our canteens, and shared suntan lotion. With so many of us on the Mall already and more marching in, it was a carnival—I got choked up at everyone smiling and hugging. The optimism and excitement rippled through us all. They had to notice a force this strong, right? At that moment I felt accepted, energized and, most importantly, resilient. I wanted to stay that way for the rest of my life. It was clear what I had to do.

The next day, April 26, 1993, I handed in my resignation to Westinghouse Defense and Electronic Systems. I've been out and happy ever since.

The start of the 1993 March on Washington.

Bob Angell (he/him)'s work has appeared in Asimov's Science Fiction, Interzone, Gargoyle, The Baltimore Review, *and many anthologies including* Best Date Ever: True Stories That Celebrate Gay Relationships. *His LGBTQ YA VR AI SF romantic thriller,* Best Game Ever, *was published in May 2019 under the name R R Angell. Bob is honored that his long-time friend, Frank M. Robinson (who was Harvey Milk's speechwriter), wrote his memoir* Not So Good A Gay Man *as a letter to Bob, and Bob was able to write the "Afterward." More at rrangell.com*

Fire Island's Most Notorious Guest

By Charles Baran-Bookman

I WAS AN EXCELLENT HOUSEBOY at first. Mondays I'd do the laundry: sheets in the morning, towels in the afternoon. Tuesdays I'd vacuum and shake the sand out of the area rugs. Wednesdays I'd clean the three bathrooms. On Thursday I'd grocery shop for the weekend. By 4 p.m., I was done.

I then took a quick jump in the pool and headed over to Tea Dance and sat on the railing, watching the parade of beautiful bronzed Fire Island men come and go as I sipped my Blue Whale.

At first, Tea Dance was an after-work ritual; not an obsession. But my houseboy duties and schedule began to deteriorate rapidly by mid-July. I'd cram everything, cleaning, cooking, and laundry into Friday morning, finishing literally minutes before the guys walked off the ferry. The Fire Island social scene became my main obsession. I was a fixture at every Tea Dance along with other Pines' regulars, like Lady B, a four foot overly tanned woman somewhere between 55 and 85 years old. No one knew, or dared to ask, her age.

Lady B would show up at Tea Dance in a bikini top hanging perilously low on her emaciated chest, a piece of thin batik fabric barely covering her private parts, and a floppy straw hat with holes in it. She never wore shoes. She was already drunk, waving an empty Moët bottle in the air and screaming in an accent that could either be from France or from Canarsie, "I'm LADY B!"

In mid-July, I asked a bartender who she was.

"Her?" he asked, barely glancing up. "She's Trude Heller's lover."

"She's fabulous," I replied.

He chuckled and continued rinsing out glasses.

Trude Heller owned the famous Trude Heller's disco in the West Village. She was also a producer, most notably producing the 1965 Supremes Concert at Lincoln Center. I never saw Heller, the owner of the namesake West Village disco, on Fire Island, but Lady B was always at Tea. Lady B lived in Trude's house on the ocean. It was easy to figure out which house it was by the empty champagne bottles littering the beach. Lady B would just hurl them off the deck.

I had to meet her. One Wednesday afternoon, neighboring houseboy Billy and I were smoking joints when I suggested I dress up as Lady B and go to tea. He thought it was a great idea, and we quickly got an outfit together that very closely resembled her signature look. I wore a tube top, John's hat with the flowers, and two dish towels pinned around my waist.

"Ugh! I don't have a champagne bottle. The empty Chardonnay bottles just laying around aren't right," I whined.

"I'll be back!" Billy said as he ran to his house. I looked out the kitchen window and saw him rummaging through the trash cans on the board walk. In no time he was back with an empty, if slightly soiled, bottle of Asti Spumante.

As we walked to Tea, I was nervous. My heart was pounding. Lady B was formidable, and I didn't want to mess with her. I prayed she would find my impersonation humorous. I certainly didn't want to go home with a lump on my head from an empty Moet bottle.

The crowd was thick that afternoon. Billy and I couldn't see Lady B as we made our way up the steps, but she was there, roaring, "I'm LADY B!!" over and over again from somewhere deep in the crowd.

She sounded exceptionally inebriated. My costume was recognized as I moved through the crowd. People started nudging each other and I heard someone say, "Oh, look. There's another Lady B."

The six or seven men directly in front of her parted when they saw me coming, giving us a direct path. Then someone nudged her, and Lady B stopped screaming. She turned around, looked at me and stared.

"Who the hell are you??" she yelled.

My answer, totally unrehearsed, came to me in a flash.

"I'm Lady A! If You're Lady B, then I'm Lady A!" I screamed.

The crowd gasped. Everyone stopped talking, waiting for Lady B's reaction. All you could hear was the muffled sound of Sylvester's "You Make Me Feel Mighty Real" coming off the dance floor.

Then Lady B flung her head back and let out a huge guttural laugh. She ran over to me and threw her arms around me, spilling warm Moet over my left shoulder. I was shocked.

Shocked, yes, that the intimidating Lady B threw her arms around me and loved the joke, but even more shocked because the bottle wasn't empty after all.

The author in the 1980s at Fire Island.

Charles Baran-Bookman is the author of Rhoda Rage and the Goldfish Letter, *an LGBTQ+ cozy mystery set in Wilton Manors, Florida, and published by Line by Lion Publications. An actor and senior writer for South Florida's* OutClique Magazine, *Charles and his husband Kirk Bookman will soon celebrate 37 glorious years together.*

Visibility

By Sarah Priestman

My son's tattoo—"visible," in Times New Roman on his right forearm —was a present from me for his 18th birthday. He is transgender, and to him, visibility is an antidote to stigma; it's refusing what most of the world still wants trans people to do: disappear. With this word on his sleeve (his skin, really), he claims the power of being seen. It is his visibility, and not mine, but being his mother has allowed me to also choose to be seen. And isn't this what we all want? To be seen for who we are?

My son came out as trans his freshman year of high school, after identifying as genderqueer in middle school. I believed then that being transgender meant having a bull's eye on your back, which for some— especially trans women of color—it can. I was afraid. Since he'd shopped in the boys' department and stuck with a short haircut throughout his childhood, I'd assumed he'd eventually identify as gay. Be whomever you want to be, I'd told him. Listen to what's true for you. I had danced at countless queer bars, so the possibility of having a gay child felt—dare I say it—"normal." Being transgender, however, felt like a risk.

I could not have known, then, that within a few years I would bask in his having the gall to live candidly. I watched him become an advocate. He wrote articles, gave speeches, mentored LGBT students. I saw his visibility illuminating a path for other transitioning kids, still in the shadows.

A mother in a support group whose son had transitioned a year before made me feel more comfortable and less afraid.

"I now see that this is who he was all along," she said. "Transitioning allowed him to be who he really is."

Maybe this is who my son really is, I thought.

I'd had plenty of clues, but when Evie was younger, I'd not been willing to listen. A neighbor told me about meeting him in kindergarten, when he confided, "I'm a boy." I'd been comfortable with his choosing a neck ties for elementary school pictures, but I cringe to remember my response when he begged to be called "John" on a beach trip, aching to be recognized as the boy he knew he was. He wore baggy surfer shorts and a swim shirt. I only saw a girl, pretending to be a boy. Calling him a boy's name felt like this was no longer an imaginary game. "No way," I'd said, collecting the towels and umbrella and marching toward the car as if ending this day trip would end the discussion. A decade later, he described this disconnect in a TEDx Talk entitled, "It Takes a Village to Transition."

"Transgender individuals are often asked when they realized they were not a boy or not a girl," he said. "But this doesn't make sense to all of us." While other tomboys became more feminine as they got older, he explained, "I knew inside that I was a boy all along, and now I just wanted to live like one."

Many parents hear their trans or gender nonconforming kids tell their truth, and they recoil, or deny, instead of listening. My son's courage taught me to not only listen, but also to learn about what it takes to be brave enough to be seen as who one truly is.

As parents, we often push our kids. Sometimes it's for top-of-the-class grades, or to excel in sports or the arts. We then behave as if their accomplishments are ordinary—even assumed—when they succeed.

Neither makes sense to me. I didn't push Evie to be an advocate, nor do I pretend to be modest. Instead, I revel in his bravery. When I joined him in his truth, it was an opportunity for me to be visible in my truth, as well: a mother who's love for her son allows her to learn from his courage.

One year, for the local pride parade, my son tied a transgender flag around his shoulders, letting it float behind him like a cape. It was a steamy day in June. The year he wore his cape it was so hot that I watched from an air-conditioned bar, waving as he walked by, his pink, blue and white striped flag buoyant, visible in a sea of superheroes.

AUTHOR'S BIOGRPHY NEXT PAGE

Sarah Priestman has an MFA in Creative Writing from American University, and held residencies at the Cummington Colony for the Arts, Virginia Center for the Creative Arts, and the Bread Loaf Writers' Conference. Her work has been published in The Hudson Review, Entropy, Cutthroat: A Journal of the Arts, Common Boundary, *and* Washingtonian. *Essays have been recognized in* Best American Essays, *honored for Literary Excellence by the DC Commission on the Arts and Humanities and the Barry Lopez Nonfiction Award, and nominated for a Pushcart Prize. https://sarahpriestman.com/*

Protecting

A sailor in Spain in 1992 survives military witch hunts with a friend's help. A California mother struggles to protect her trans son. An American trans woman recovering from surgery in Thailand identifies with Frankenstein's monster. These stories challenge the idea of protection as a strategy to maintain the status quo, focusing instead on the ways in which we protect each other when we are at our most vulnerable, when we don't know how to protect ourselves.

A Day in Hyderabad's Flower Market

By Patruni Sastry

IT WAS 5 AM ON A SUNDAY and I was up early, preparing myself for what would be one of the most unconventional days of my life. I started my day by sipping a cup of tea while applying makeup, multitasking between the warmth of the tea and the cool touch of primer and moisturizer. My partner and child were still deep in sleep, their rhythmic breathing calming my nerves as I painted my face. Normally, drag makeup is a process done later in the day or evening, when the world is awake and bustling. But here I was, transforming myself at an ungodly hour, layering foundation, contour, lenses, and lashes. It felt as unnatural as eating Hyderabadi biryani for breakfast, yet there was something exhilarating about it.

I'd never stepped out of my home in full drag before. Hyderabad, despite its progress in many areas, remains conservative when it comes to accepting identities like mine. Drag queens don't always feel safe in this city, and stepping out in public in full glam was a risk. But I was willing to take it for this shoot. I had watched enough Bollywood movies to know that a good pair of sunglasses could shield both my identity and my makeup from prying eyes. I packed my carefully chosen outfit—flowers handcrafted by my partner, and a wig—into a bag, locked the door behind me, and called an Uber.

The driver greeted me as "bhaiya," not realizing that in less than an hour, he would be transporting someone who looked entirely different. As we drove through the still-dark streets of Hyderabad, I asked him to stop midway to pick up Manab, my friend and photographer. We had known each other since our school days in Kharagpur, and both of us had come a long way from those simpler times. Now, we were collaborating on something new, something bold and artistic. We were planning a public drag photoshoot, a venture that felt both exhilarating and terrifying, especially in a city that wasn't used to seeing queerness, or drag queens, out in the open.

Our destination was Gudimalkhapur, South India's largest flower market, an hour away from where I lived. The market opens early in the morning, bustling with vendors selling fresh flowers in bulk for everything from weddings to funerals. There was no place for me to change at the market, so I did my makeup and final touches in the car, my hands trembling slightly as we neared our destination. Once we arrived, I found a small corner near a public toilet where I could discreetly slip into my saree, corset, and wig.

The moment I stepped into the market, everything changed. The smell of fresh flowers—roses, jasmine, marigold—filled the air, mingling with the sound of trucks loading and unloading, vendors shouting, and auto rickshaws honking. As I walked, I could feel eyes on me, following me with a mixture of curiosity and confusion. People stopped mid-conversation to stare, their gazes lingering as I moved past. I could almost hear their thoughts: "What is this?"

Manab and I started the photoshoot near a stack of flower baskets freshly unloaded from a truck. He clicked away as people gathered around us, watching closely. Some stared in silent curiosity, while others became bold enough to follow us as we moved from one part of the market to another. We asked shopkeepers for permission to take photos near their stalls, and most agreed, intrigued by the spectacle of a drag queen in the middle of their flower-filled world.

But soon, a small crowd began to form around us. Vendors and passersby stopped what they were doing, their curiosity turning into something more confrontational. In a matter of minutes, we were surrounded by ten to fifteen people, some of them demanding that we stop what we were doing. The tension in the air was palpable, and for a moment, I felt a pang of fear. It was a reminder that queerness and gender nonconformity are still met with resistance in many places, even in a space as seemingly neutral as a flower market.

The crowd started asking for our camera, insisting that we didn't have permission to take photos there. Manab, ever protective of his equipment, stood his ground. Sensing the situation escalating, I decided to step in. They assumed we didn't speak the local language and thought I was a foreigner. That's when I switched to Telugu, explaining who we were and what we were trying to do. In a quick elevator pitch, I introduced them to the basics of gender and drag, hoping to disarm their suspicion.

After a tense few minutes, the market secretary stepped in. He listened to our explanation, and to our relief, he granted us permission to continue our shoot, as long as we didn't disrupt the vendors' business. With this newfound approval, we moved more freely, taking photos in more dramatic locations, capturing the chaotic beauty of the market alongside the fluidity of my drag persona.

My costume for the shoot was a blend of Victorian and Indian influences. I wore a white saree adorned with oversized, dramatic flowers, a black leather corset, and a golden cape that trailed behind me. The wig I wore cascaded down my shoulders in a wave of curls, and my entire look was designed to evoke the opulence of a bygone era, fused with a sense of queerness that transcended time and place. I felt like a character out of a Shakespearean play, walking through the market as if it were a stage, with the flower vendors and customers serving as my audience.

The flowers around me took on a deeper meaning as we continued the shoot. Flowers have long been symbols of desire, sexuality, and hidden meanings, especially in queer culture. In the Victorian era, floriography—the language of flowers—allowed people to communicate their emotions and desires in ways that society wouldn't permit them to say out loud. A white rose might symbolize innocence, but paired with a dark violet, it became a symbol of hidden passion.

The white flowers on my saree were meant to symbolize purity, but their exaggerated size turned that symbolism on its head. They were unapologetically large, just like the queer experience itself—impossible to ignore, unwilling to be silenced. As I stood among the stalls, the scent of jasmine and roses filling the air, I felt like I was part of something bigger, a living testament to the fluidity of identity and the defiance of societal norms.

For this shoot, Manab and I had drawn inspiration from Shakespearean themes of gender fluidity and transformation. In plays like A Midsummer Night's Dream, flowers are not just decoration; they are potions of change, capable of revealing hidden desires and disrupting societal norms. Similarly, drag is a form of transformation, a way of expressing fluidity in a world that often tries to box us into rigid categories.

After about three hours of shooting, we decided to wrap up. I found the same corner near the public toilet where I had changed earlier and began transforming back into my everyday self. By the time I finished, I was no longer the drag queen who had turned heads in the market, but just another person waiting for an Uber. As I sipped chai with Manab and reflected on the day, we talked about the microaggressions we had faced, but also about how powerful it felt to claim space, to demand attention, and to create art in a place that wasn't ready for us.

When I finally arrived home, my partner and child were still asleep. I washed the makeup off my face, slipped into bed beside them, and allowed myself a couple of hours of rest. As I drifted off to sleep, I smiled, knowing that for a moment, in the heart of Hyderabad's flower market, I had been something more than just a drag queen—I had been a living symbol of queerness blooming in a world not yet ready for it. ❧

The author during their photoshoot in a flower marker in Hyderabad. The costume is of both Indian and Victorian influences, including a black leather corset, a golden cape, and a floral dress.

Patruni Sastry is an expressionist dancer, performance artist, and Tranimal Drag performer. Patruni started dancing at the age of seven and uses "Expressionism" to tell stories of awareness to society. Patruni performs dance and drag in many national and international venues, promoting avant-garde art, anti-beauty themes, and a postmodern approach to art, sometimes with dance and other times with folk music. They have performed in more than 1000 shows, 50 workshops, five TEDx talks, as well as fashion walks and digital performances across all mediums.

The Friend Who Stayed

By Daniel Hendrick

"**I'VE GOT SOME BAD NEWS,**" the lieutenant commander began, pointing to a seat across from her desk. I sat down, trying not to look nervous despite the deepening pit in my stomach. It was the early morning of Tuesday, May 26, 1992. I was 21 years old.

I knew exactly what the commander would say, why she had summoned me to her windowless office as I was coming off back-to-back overnight shifts. This was the moment I had been dreading for two months after agents from the Naval Investigative Service questioned me about John, a Marine I had a crush on whom I thought was gay. Unfortunately, this foreknowledge did nothing to stem the tide of panic and dread swelling inside me.

"NIS has concluded its investigation and determined that there are grounds to suspect you are a homosexual. You are being recommended for separation from military service," she said, pausing for a few seconds for a response that never came. "I recommended getting good legal counsel and taking these next few days to think about what you will do. Do you have any questions?"

"No, ma'am."

"Very well. Your security clearance is revoked until the matter is closed. You will be reassigned to Facilities in 30-F. I'll need to take your badge. You'll get a new one when you come back later this week."

I stood up, handed her the badge and opened the door. I walked briskly toward the exit, past the sentry desk where I used to stand watch, and stepped out into the morning sun.

As I continued toward the front gate, I gazed up at the towering antennas that formed the "Bullring" of the Navy listening post where I was stationed in Rota, Spain. My head was spinning so fast that I don't remember much about the next few days, except for biking to my off-base housing as fast I could, as if trying to outrun my truth one last time.

I knew immediately that a new life was dawning, one of wrenching decisions, military proceedings and searching for the words to tell my family: Not only am I gay but I am being kicked out of the Navy for it.

What I hadn't counted on was feeling completely abandoned. When I returned to the Bullring a few days later, an admin handed me a red badge to replace the green one the commander took away. I no longer had access to the secure watch floor where I worked for the last year as an enlisted cryptologist. Instead, I reported to 30-F where I mopped floors, painted decks, and fixed things for the next four months. I was even required to have an escort accompany to me to the restroom.

Just like Hester Prynne, my new badge signaled a major transgression for all to pass their judgment—only instead of Hester's scarlet "A" for adultery, my red badge telegraphed "G" for gay.

"What happened to Petty Officer Hendrick?""Why did they take away his security clearance?""Why is he in 30-F?""Holy shit."

In a matter of hours, shipmates who were normally friendly ducked into side rooms to avoid me in the passageways. My old supervisors would only nod from a safe distance. In the cafeteria, not a soul would make eye contact. So much for the intelligence community keeping secrets: Everyone knew.

The toughest part was being left to fight alone by other gay servicemembers, most of whom now avoided me like the plague. In retrospect, it was impossible to blame them, for they were now at tremendous risk of guilt by association. All of my actions, all of my relationships, came under a microscope in the weeks leading up to my administrative trial. I later reviewed my official case file and read depositions of friends and co-workers who were questioned about my personal relationships. The authorities were hoping to ensnare others in their witch hunt.

In a matter of days, I became a complete pariah. I was desperate to find a way out, but couldn't tell my family. I wrote to my Senator back home, Carl Levin, but he didn't respond. Not only was I facing military prosecution, not only did I have no money to hire a private attorney or know how to find organizations to help, not only did I have to confront my shame about being gay and now getting booted out of the military; I was crushingly alone.

Except for one friend.

It's hard to overstate the risk Randy took later that week when he walked over to the maintenance shed where I spent most work days trying to avoid the world. In plain view of the Facilities staff and everyone passing by—and at a time when every aspect of my life was under scrutiny—he came over to say hello. "Hey Dano. Whatcha doin'?"

Randy and I had known each other for a couple of years, having overlapped foreign language training in California. We had a lot in common: both good at learning languages, both from Michigan, and both trying to navigate gay life in the deeply homophobic military of the 1990s.

We were members of a small group who used to leave base on the weekends to visit gay bars in Seville, located a safe two-hour drive away. Unlike most of the others, however, Randy wasn't afraid to be seen with me—on base or at work, defiantly. We began to hang out more and more, whether for dinner or visiting nearby towns. We started lifting weights a couple of times a week at the base gym—sometimes just steps away from the very Marine who turned me in. "That's him? I mean, he's okay," Randy said, when I pointed out John. Then, turning his head over to another guy in a tight shirt and shorts on the bench press: "Now that one over there, he's really hot."

Randy saw me in a way that I needed to be seen because he had been there himself. Randy had been investigated—I suspect more than once—because he was more comfortable in his own skin, more out than I was at the time. "You know what, if they ask me again, I'll just tell them and get out. I've had enough of this bullshit."

Randy's acts of solidarity and courage decades ago almost certainly saved my life. They also laid the foundation for a friendship that is still my closest. In the intervening decades, after getting thrown out of the Navy, we became very close, more like brothers than friends.

There's a saying that "An old friend is worth two new ones." When it comes to longtime queer friends, the ones who have lived the same struggles and walked through the fire with you, their true value is priceless.

Daniel Hendrick is the author of Jamaica Bay, *a history book about the New York City estuary, and the producer and writer of* Saving Jamaica Bay, *a documentary film narrated by Susan Sarandon. Dan is currently finishing his first novel.*

Our Brush with Italy's Liberation

By George De Stefano

In July 2000, my partner Rob and I spent several weeks in Italy, beginning in Rome. We came to the Eternal City for World Pride Roma, a week of gay cultural and political activities culminating in a march. The event attracted several hundred thousand gay men, lesbians, trans people, and heterosexual allies, from Italy and abroad. But World Pride, an international celebration held in a different capital city each year, almost didn't make it to Rome. The Vatican and its conservative political allies waged a vituperative, unabashedly bigoted campaign to prevent it from being held in Rome in 2000, the year of the Giubileo, the Catholic Church's millennial Holy Year celebration.

The opposition to World Pride Roma backfired; it ended up generating an outpouring of support from Italians who believed that the attempts to ban it constituted an assault on the Constitution and lo stato laico, the secular state. Support came from a wide range of public figures, from the president of Rome's Jewish community to artists such as filmmaker Nanni Moretti and the playwright Dario Fo, as well as from liberal and leftist political parties, civil society organizations, trade unions, and even grassroots Catholic associations that condemned the Vatican's stance. The leftist newspaper Il Manifesto published a statement of solidarity titled, "Siamo tutti gay" ("We are all gay").

World Pride Roma 2000 was a great success. Its significance, however, was greater than the size of the crowds or even the defeat of its formidable foes. What the event signaled was the refusal of the gay population—or at least its activists—to accept the unfavorable terms of the social contract offered by Italian society. Male and female homosexual behavior has been legal in Italy since 1890. Italy does not have sodomy laws, and the age of consent is fourteen, for both hetero- and homosexuals.

The absence of legal prohibitions, however, didn't mean there was no stigma or discrimination. Catholicism may no longer be Italy's official state religion, but its influence remains pervasive. Social attitudes towards homosexuality are strongly influenced by the Church's stance that it is both sinful and unnatural, and that gay people should be tolerated only as long as they suffer their condition in silence and don't demand civil rights or social acceptance.

In 2000, there were no anti-discrimination laws in Italy (employment discrimination was banned in 2003), and it wasn't until 2016 that same-sex civil unions became legal. At the dawn of the 21st century, Italy was very much the land of "Don't ask, don't tell." Don't tell your friends, your coworkers, your schoolmates, and above all your family. (It would kill your mother! Given how often I've heard that one, Italian mothers must be a very fragile species indeed.)

World Pride challenged this societal omertà. "In Italy, invisibility has been the price for tolerance," observed Sergio Lo Giudice, at that time the president of Aricgay, the national gay rights association. "But gays don't want to be invisible anymore."

While in Rome, we met up with Salvo, a friend who had come from Sicily to march in World Pride. As we stepped off the sidewalk to join the marchers, Salvo, with tears in his eyes, said, "You have no idea how much this means to us."

Two weeks later, Rob and I went to Sicily to visit him and two other friends, Gianni and Salvone. The couple had planned a trip for the four of us in Selinunte, an ancient, picturesque town of Greek and Phoenician origins on the island's west coast. After the long drive from Catania, the main city of eastern Sicily, we arrived at our hotel. As we were checking in, there was a problem. Gianni had reserved two rooms with double beds, for Rob and me, and for him and Salvone. But the clerk decided that four men could not have accommodations with the letto matrimoniale, literally the "marriage bed." He insisted we take rooms with single beds. Gianni refused to accept this. The conversation escalated into an argument, with rising decibels and growing frustration on both sides. Gianni, a university professor from an upper-middle-class family, code-switched from his usual polished Italian to the more emphatic Sicilian dialect. The clerk's boss emerged from his office, quickly assessed the situation, and then told his underling, "Let them have what they want."

Word of Gianni's intervention, and our presence, spread at the hotel. Our clearly gay waiter in the hotel's restaurant was notably friendly and solicitous. A British family at a nearby table, enjoying their meal, was oblivious to the fact that their teenage son was smiling and winking at us.

Back in New York City, after an eventful Italian sojourn that began in Rome and ended in Sicily, we received an e-mail from Gianni. He said that he and Salvone enjoyed the time the four of us spent together and that they looked forward to seeing us again. Then he put the confrontation with the hotel desk clerk at Selinunte in a different and surprising light. It turned out that the success of World Pride Roma, and the example of Rob's and my openness about our sexuality, had encouraged Gianni to challenge the disapproving clerk.

"Thank you," he said, "for bringing some of the spirit of World Pride to Sicily."

Rob Eisdorfer, left, and his partner, writer George De Stefano.

George De Stefano is a writer and editor living in Queens, New York, with his spouse, Rob. He is the author of An Offer We Can't Refuse: The Mafia in the Mind of America *and is a contributing author of many other titles. His articles and reviews have appeared in numerous print and online publications.*

Sympathy for "The Monster"

By Leith Angel Johnson

Dj, MY 14-YEAR-OLD SON, is disappointed. He and I are discussing *Frankenstein; or The Modern Prometheus.*

"There isn't, like, a bunch of blood or dead body parts?" he asks. "No, not really," I say.

DJ looks exceptionally disheartened to hear this.

"Does anybody get killed, at least?" he asks. "Oh, yeah," I say. "Lots of people." My son's eyes light up again.

Pretty much everything DJ knows about Mary Shelley's *Frankenstein*, originally published in 1818, was learned by watching the iconic, flat-headed monster grunting and lurching about in the classic horror movies by Universal Studios. But these types of films, with their forbidding castles, hunchbacked assistants, and bandaged cadavers waiting to be brought back to life by bolts of lightning, are more indicative of a Frankenstein-ish genre that is altogether distinct from any imagery presented in Shelley's novel.

As a teenager during the 1980s, I eagerly sat through three back-to-back screenings of *The Bride*, starring Sting as Doctor Frankenstein and *Flash Dance*'s Jennifer Beal as his gorgeous and (somewhat) feminist female creation. Then, on Saturday nights, I pulled on a corset and garters to sing and dance on stage during midnight screenings of *The Rocky Horror Picture Show* as Dr. Frank N. Furter cooed to the audience, "Don't dream it, be it."

What little I did know about Mary Shelley's time in Geneva, where she conceived her story during the spring of 1816, I learned from *Gothic*, a 1986 New Wave horror flick, in which Shelley's sensitive, yet sexy blonde husband, Percy, locks lips with a dangerous and darkly handsome Lord Byron. Once the clock strikes midnight in *Frankenstein*-inspired films like these, we're beckoned to leave our daylight inhibitions behind and give in to our darkest, most erotic fantasies beneath the sensuous light of a blood-red moon.

More recently, and well into the age of genetic engineering, artificial intelligence, and nanotechnology, *Frankenstein*, more often than not, inspires horror films like 2009's *Splice*, in which a genetic engineer named Elsa (after Elsa Lanchester, the actress who played the bride in Universal Pictures' *Bride of Frankenstein*) splices together human and animal DNA to create a new hybrid creature that—spoiler alert!—transitions from female to male, and then proceeds to rape and impregnate its creator. Here, the story at least adheres to the novel's cautionary theme of human as creator in which Victor Frankenstein, in the name of scientific discovery, attempts to usurp the power of God by "infusing life into an inanimate body," but winds up unleashing his creation's "insatiable thirst for vengeance" upon the world, instead.

Still, *Frankenstein* can seemingly be made to mean just about anything, from a slave narrative to a metaphor for postpartum depression. After reading the novel myself, I concluded that the main message Mary Shelley sought to impart is that "monsters" are created when someone is discriminated against because of a socially constructed difference, such as race, class, or sexual orientation. Indeed, even my own personal story played out within the novel's pages: that of being transgender.

Like the many landscapes depicted in Shelley's novel, Thailand is also renowned for its natural beauty. Nonetheless, on the morning when I was wheeled into a hospital operating room for my gender reassignment surgery, I could very well have been hidden away on the secluded island where Victor Frankenstein labored over his second creature, instead of Phuket.

Sanguan Kunaporn, my surgeon, greeted me, looking every measure the mad scientist in his surgical gown, apron, and cap. He was seated at a desk and positioned above a light box, which cast shadows across his face, giving him a somewhat demonic appearance. In one latex-gloved hand, he held what looked to be a semi-translucent sac of some sort. In his other hand, he pinched a threaded needle. He was slowly and methodically stitching the sides of the pouch together.

"Hello, Leith," Dr. Sanguan said to me, his voice muffled beneath his surgeon's mask. "I'm preparing your vagina, now." That scene remains the most surreal experience of my life.

Like many trans people, particularly prior to transitioning, Frankenstein's creature is acutely aware of the dichotomy that exists between his internal reality and outward physical presentation. "I cherished hope, it is true," he says, "but it vanished, when I beheld my person reflected in water."

This awareness of his nonconforming physicality also prevents him from approaching the family he has observed for months through the "small and almost imperceptible chink" that exists between his shelter and their cottage. "What chiefly struck me was the gentle manners of these people," the creature says, describing the cottagers, "and I longed to join them, but dared not." Repeated rejection has taught him that where others "ought to see a feeling and kind friend, they behold only a detestable monster"—a familiar refrain for trans folk, and the reason why determining whether or not to enter a public washroom, or disclose one's gender identity status to friends, healthcare providers, or a potential intimate partner always requires careful deliberation.

Still, to situate the creature's story solely in this context is, admittedly, far too constrained. Frankenstein's creature is, after all, nameless. As such, his story belongs to anyone who has ever felt "irrevocably excluded," for whatever reason. While Victor Frankenstein clearly suffers great loss, it is the creature that suffers the most.

"Blasted as thou wert, my agony was still superior to thine," the creature says, addressing Victor's corpse as Shelley's novel draws to a close. "But soon," he continues, "I shall die, and what I now feel be no longer felt."

The creature's final sentiment is, unfortunately, also familiar. Each year, the trans community gathers together "on a dreary night of November" for Transgender Day of Remembrance. This is when, "by the glimmer of the half-extinguished light" of our own candles, we recall the trans folk who have died during the preceding twelve months, either of their own volition or violently at the hands of others, simply because someone considered them monstrous.

Leith Angel, aka Riftgirl, is the author of Being T: The Riftgirl Blog, *a widely-read blog about her experiences living and dating as a single trans woman during the early 2000s. Her videos and performances have been shown at international women's and 2SLGBTQ events, and her essays, interviews, and comics have appeared in various print and online publications.*

Gay Heroes
I Have Known

By William Lawrence

My FIRST CONNECTION with people and organizations that campaigned for gay rights was my introduction to the Albany Trust in the UK. I was a teenager at the time, when a well-meaning teacher of drama came to my rescue. He had spotted that my eyes tended to drift toward the male figures in the dramatic line up and he was also aware that my father had recently thrown me out on the street for wearing shirts with frilly cuffs—very avant-garde in the mid '60's. So, being the good hearted bloke that my teacher was, he promptly helped me find somewhere safe to stay and took me personally along to the Albany Trust for support.

In a world that seems to emphasize the cynical, we must try to remember there are a lot of good and kind people out there who are willing to put themselves on the line for the sake of a noble cause that only asks for equal rights and decent interaction.

The gentleman at the Albany Trust suggested I attend a regular gathering of young gay men. I say men, but the fact was, we were all in our mid to late teens, boys really—but boys who felt oppressed by a harsh system that was only too willing to call us "poofs" and pillow biters" and tended to kick our heads in, especially if we were a little fey.

The group was run by Richard and Denis. The latter was Denis Lemon, founder and editor of *Gay News*. The couple had well-appointed digs off High Street Kensington. Once a week, a bunch of young dudes would meet at their place, be served coffee and biscuits, and allowed to be themselves. This was a wonderful time for me, sharing and endlessly chatting with others without worrying if the glint in my eye might be misinterpreted, and meet with a sharp punch!

This was the first part of my liberation. I had passionate conversations and passionate sex.

My next encounter with activists happened by chance when I attended my first meeting of the Gay Liberation movement in the UK, which took place in a basement in some building in the center of London. It was a raucous event with lots of cheering, lots of drag, and lots of excitement. I had been taken there by a school mate, Julian Hows, who now works for GNP: the Global Network of People living with AIDS. I remember he caused quite a stir once by turning up in the playground dressed in a skirt. He was a brave individual even then. But that was over fifty years ago, and, like so many exceptional acts, it is now lost in the tide of time.

Not long after that I met another equally daring young man, Peter Burton, who went on to help establish the gay magazine *Jeremy*. It was the first highbrow mag with literary commentary by famous writers, albeit sitting alongside well-formed pecs and ample packages. Peter Burton had started his campaign of poking literary giants out of the closet.

Then came Robin Maugham. Robin—who was to become my mentor, friend, and lover—had been pushing the envelope since his first famous publication, *The Servant*. In the novella he explores the homoerotic relationship between Tony, the master and Barrett his servant; however, the servant's assistant with whom the master becomes entangled and eventually rapes, was originally intended to be a boy—but in those days, the 1940's, he didn't dare risk the controversy; you can read between the lines.

Then, in 1958, he finished *The Wrong People*, set in Tangier, which was explicit and uncompromising in its sexual content, however dark. His uncle, Somerset Maugham, who read the book in one sitting, told him not to attempt publication, or else: "They'll murder you!" The story exposed the under-belly of the sex trafficking of young boys within the context of a simply told narrative.

When I first met Robin Maugham at the tender age of nineteen, I had little idea of his passion and determination to break the slave cartels of sub-Saharan Africa. I wasn't even aware that this had been the subject of his Maiden Speech in the House of Lords. The only indication I had that he was involved in any campaign at all was when, at a soirée in Knightsbridge thrown by the society photographer Allan Warren, I had an encounter with the musical genius Lionel Bart.

"Come and meet the magical Lionel Bart," Allan said.

A crumpled figure in a long dark coat sidled toward me, followed by a jostling stream of gleaming wannabes from his recent musical. I knew the composer's face. I had seen him interviewed on television about his brilliant work *Oliver*. He was a friend of Robin's and must have been told I was his new personal assistant, because of his opening line—which he said so quietly that I could hardly hear him—was: "You know, Robin should never have used the word 'bollocks' in that interview for the BBC. It was over the top."

At the time I didn't have a clue what he was talking about. But, as I was to find out later, my partner had only just been interviewed by Sheridan Morley in the BBC's *Late-Night Line Up* program, in which he had openly admitted his attraction to men. The big deal was the fact that Robin had been the first member of the House of Lords to talk openly about his sexual orientation: "I love boys as much as girls and anybody who didn't understand that bisexuality was a natural condition was talking bollocks!" he had told the startled interviewer.

In my life have met many people who have been examples of fearless campaigning, including Christopher Isherwood—but that's a story for another day. Therefore, when the HIV/AIDS epidemic hit hard in the early '90s and I lost two former lovers to the virus, I had no hesitation but to go on my own crusade. I wrote a play titled *Never Walk Alone*. With the support of many dedicated AIDS organizations, the drama toured schools, colleges, and universities. My hope is that its safe-sex message made a difference and helped the young people, as I had been helped so many years before.

The author in the early 1970s.

Following the successful tour of his AIDS awareness drama, Never Walk Alone, and the run of Blue on Blue at the Edinburgh Festival Fringe, William Lawrence now presents his musical, Morgan's Ghost, at the Stables Theatre in Hastings, UK. Set in a curio shop, the production offers a critique of empire wrapped in a love story during the heyday of piracy. Web: williamlawrence.co.uk

Parenting My Genderfluid Child

By Caitlin Billings

As a first-time mother, I endured the earnest "May god be with you" prayers of my parents' generation. When my kids were teenagers, our home would become the cool space where kids could hang out, curse, and watch gritty streaming content. Intellectual discourse about feminism, chemistry, and beat poetry united the generations. As parents, we were readu for anything what with our vegan, gender-neutral household.

Enter reality. At twelve, our oldest child developed a restricted eating disorder. A few months later it seemed we'd done the right thing with early intervention, but I was called back to the school. My half-grown adolescent and I sat together on a small couch across from the school counselor and she shared her observations. There were incidents of cutting, a suicide attempt, and a hospitalization.

My husband and I spent the next two years reeling from our oldest child going from one newfound identity to another: as bisexual, agender, genderluid, nonbinary. And amid these pronouncements: "I was sexually abused."

I wish I could write that I did not conflate sexual abuse with my teen's gender identity and what the psychiatric field so dubiously refers to as "gender dysphoria." Homosexuality, also once a psychiatric condition, was blamed on various factors: sexual abuse, overbearing mothers, weak or absent fathers, and so on. But today's affirming websites teemed with information and images that my genderfluid peers once had longed for, just clicks away from my child's keen eyes.

My fourteen-year-old had come out as trans. I dutifully ordered a chest binder, appalled to discover later that my teen hadn't taken it off since putting it on for the first time. "You can't do that," I said. "The directions said so. No sleeping in the binder!"

This could have been humorous, but I focused on my new belief that sexual assault by a family member had changed my beautiful girl into a depressed, hostile, gender-questioning kid. I thought I was doing Avery (his chosen name) a favor by supporting (secretly tolerating) his new gender expression. My psychoanalytic revelation was that, because a man had harmed Avery, he wanted to become a man to protect himself. It seemed to make so much sense.

I cried a lot during that time, partly because my trans child's biological sex had made him prey to the pedophile lurking in our family. But also because I wanted to save Avery from the horror that is a sexual assault by welcoming my teenager into the circle of female survivors. How I wanted to fill my child with love and empowerment, and instill a healthy fear of men. One had betrayed me when I said no, after all. I knew the drill.

When my teenager came out as trans-male, I blamed myself. I blamed exposure to the family pedophile and the Internet and peer influence and the educational system. The progressive public middle school we had chosen for our kids now seemed suspect.

I wish I hadn't been afraid to attend the local support group advertised for parents of trans teens in our community. Maybe I would have discovered that my responses were not unusual. I was not the only parent who took out the photo albums after bedtime and wept. My grief was not something to be ashamed of, and nobody would assume I was transphobic because I didn't want my child to be trans.

I didn't want my eldest to be male because it disrupted the entire trajectory of the life I had envisioned for him. We had raised him as a girl, and this made him vulnerable. I will not soon forget the day I had to remain outside the men's bathroom in Target, holding my hand over my mouth so I wouldn't scream in panic after Avery proudly walked inside. I was haunted by fears of rape, murder, suicide, medical problems. What if I didn't hide my despair or wasn't supportive? Raising a girl was bad enough. But raising a boy who looked like a girl who went into men's restrooms unnerved me to my core.

Since then, I have learned that Avery's gender change is not my fault. I've learned that sexual abuse was not the cause of Avery's discovery of something he had always known: that he just didn't feel comfortable as a girl. I've learned why Avery no longer wants us to call him by his "deadname." Still, the name "Avery" can't erase the day my newborn baby's warmth spread over my chest moments after birth and my husband agreed to name our daughter after a French resistance worker of importance to our family. That moment is ours, and we don't have to part with it. I've learned it's important to grieve, not because someone has died but because they have gone away and returned from a new direction.

The complicated tears I wept now make sense. Gender as a binary construct guided my upbringing and was reinforced by Second Wave feminism. Avery lived with genderfluid feelings for a very long time, but I had just found out, and it was understandably jarring. Avery hadn't planned to wear a dress to the prom, or have long hair, or sing as a mezzo-soprano. Those were my dreams, I now concede.

Avery is twenty years old, married, and lives in another country. He tells me he doesn't care what pronoun I use anymore, and he's changed his name to something less gendered and more "him." He takes testosterone but hasn't decided for how long he'll continue. His appearance, he has explained to me, is performative, because gender is a performance. "I'm more comfortable with it that way," he explained. "I don't want to box myself in by insisting on a pronoun or a 'look.' I want to be comfortable in my skin, and that changes every day. It's not really that different from when you pick your outfit for the day. I just have a broader range of styles."

It's impossible to put into a few words the pride I feel for this person. Maybe our kids are teaching me what I thought I knew before we brought them into this world, or maybe these universal statements take on a whole new meaning when reflecting over the years. Good parenting, come to find out, means learning how to shut up and listen. Good parenting means applying what you've learned from your kids to your life and theirs in order to be a better human.

Caitlin Billings, a licensed clinical social worker in California, specializes in treatment and therapy for complex trauma. Her memoir, In Our Blood, *breaks the stigma around mental health professionals' own mental health.*

Hope Can Be Found in the Gayborhood

By Lenny Duncan

My name is rev. lenny duncan (they/them) and I grew up on the sidewalks of the gayborhood. I mean the gayborhood as a concept in the United States of America, but really, almost all those places personally shaped me.

I spent 1991 through 2008 in various states of houselessness across America, and as many of us know, the scenes, hangouts, and cultural gathering spots across the country for the lost, lonely, and discarded are typically your local gayborhoods. From Castro Street on Halloween, to Duval Street in Key West on New Year's Eve, to Thirteenth Street in Philly to kick off the summer with one of the largest and earliest pride festivals—not to be mistaken with Thirteenth Street in a few other places that fit the profile—there is a haven. There is a holy oasis in the urban landscape full of worker drones who pretend you don't exist and ignore your request for help or change. There is a place for people like us. Every grubby punk rock/emo, anarchist, train-hopping, jam band-following young person in America knows it.

It is the local LGBT neighborhood.

It's you.

My parents had no language, or means, to love a kid who described their gender as "angel" to their dad because that was the only non-binary being they could think of. But the gayborhood, and specifically the books I stole from Giovanni's Closet, did.

I grew up in West Philly, a black kid with a white mom. I remember as a kid, before I had a realpolitik, but after witnessing the M.O.V.E. bombings, watching armed white men tell my father just what they thought of him, his white wife, and his misbegotten children. I remember mostly just feeling sorry for my mom because she was white. This was before I understood white privilege, or why my mom was unique in her sense that her two babies would only be truly safe in their own community, and she was the one who would have to change, adjust, and live in the black community.

But other than Mom and her family, all the rest that I had encountered seemed angry for no reason, hateful, and obsessively destructive. Heavy-handed people behind desks, behind badges in my neighborhood, or the people who handed my parents their paychecks. The smiling school administrator who made me retake the standardized test because my previous score was "impossible."

In Philadelphia the color lines are invisible, but they are still there, throughout the city like a spiderweb of socioeconomic scars raked across the face of Ben Franklin and the rest of the founding "fathers." Before the enforcement went crazy after the 9/11 attacks you could see several houseless kids like me at the time spare-changing so we can go hang up on the street in the gayborhood less than ten feet from where John Hancock laid down that ol' Hancock on the Declaration of Independence, around the corner from the only public restroom open to this day, the same one Benjamin Franklin insisted was part of his property, nine blocks from one of the earliest gathering spots for LGBT people in the country.

I hope you can hear the still wistful tones I use to speak of these places, the deeds done there, the promises inherent in the documents signed in my hometown, ratified, adopted, and the true belief I will someday see the promises laid in ink in the former Carpenters Union Hall, now Independence Hall, that I could never find as a houseless Black trans kid. There are of course much more black and, dare I say, accurate depictions of Philadelphia, but I think it is important for you to know the first time I had gay sex, the first time I went down a stranger (or let one go down on me after dancing all night) the first place I realized how comfy a dress was on a Saturday night in the summer, the first time I realized I was more femme in a "them" body, was in the same place this nation was conceived, debated, and barely won. Eating out of dumpsters, couch surfing, sitting on the sidewalk all day, and annoying you as you NIMBY or DINK your way to work.

But the difference in any LGBT neighborhood is behind every exasperated teeth-sucking step-over-me was also a sweet and gentle remembrance of days when you couldn't fit anywhere, so you made a found family.

I have wandered this land and written extensively about it in essays and even a memoir, and one thing has remained true from 1991 until 2025: The safest places for the oppressed, the downtrodden, the refused, whether they be LGBT or not, have always been and always will be our neighborhoods. I'll say it again: our neighborhoods.

Our neighborhoods that are now under attack from authoritarian economic, political, and social forces. These forces are not just from outside our communities but also within. Many may think things are going to be bad, but it's going to work out for them because their wealth, class, or proximity to whiteness and heteronormativity will protect them.

Yet Obergefell is already on the chopping block. As I write this, Florida state troopers are stationed outside Pulse Nightclub to protect state highway workers as they erase the rainbow sidewalk memorial to honor the martyred and murdered that locals keep painting back on. Or as I would say to you if we were closer: "The order to the Smithsonian ain't just for black history, fool."

It's overwhelming, it's scary, and what are we to do in the face of all this? Might I suggest we do what we do best?

After the almost inevitable election results and during the deep breath America was taking from November 2024 until Inauguration Day 2025, convincing itself it won't be that bad, my partner and I asked ourselves the same questions. We live in the Hillcrest neighborhood in San Diego. We can't do everything, and we can't help everyone, but what can we do? My years in the movement called by outsiders Black Lives Matter, my organizing work during the George Floyd uprisings in Portland, Oregon, having witnessed several cities fall apart over my time in this country, my partners' invaluable organizing experience, all this wisdom over the years and we landed where we always land: Mutual aid.

We started a gathering on Tuesday mornings called Coffee and Class Solidarity. The local Donut Star on University Avenue donates fresh donuts (and a few day-old ones) every Tuesday morning. We wake up and start the coffee around 5:30 a.m. Grab the donuts, a sandwich board sign I designed, a table, and some cups, sugar, and creamer. The early item that made all the difference was a pack of Newport 100s.

Our claim to fame was that folks could stop by, have a coffee, a donut, and a smoke. A normal Tuesday morning that many of us are already so privileged to have.

Also, pro-tip: if you have a houseless neighbor who is really struggling and talking to themselves, give them a pack of smokes. Nicotine does more for late-stage schizophrenia than most modern medications; it's why mental health units are one of the few places some people can smoke in a health care facility.

That first Tuesday was slow. We got yelled at; hot coffee was thrown in our face by a neighbor who was having a really tough time in her wheelchair and was losing her leg to infection. It was my first Coffee and Class Solidarity baptism, as I call them, but we came back the next Tuesday, and the Tuesday after that.

First, it was just our houseless neighbors, but soon we were joined by a good mix of store owners, homeowners, sweet working-class queers on their way to work, organizers, and even a few "community leaders" who have tried to scare us off, accusing us of "luring the houseless."

We share a cup, concerns, conversation, and community and find something intangible yet palpable in one another's shared humanity.

Many an elder member of our community has found a home with us in a trendy neighborhood that passes them by like waste on the road. We asked people what they wanted, and now we do a lot of harm prevention, connection to services, and community defense. Our houseless neighbors, who are always more tuned into dangers in the area, share information with our other neighbors about these threats and concerns, and we even come up with shared community safety solutions. We aren't solving all their problems. We aren't even solving one on most days.

It is illegal for us to do this in San Diego, for a pastor to feed the houseless. It has inherent risk caring for these people, in a country such as this, at a time such as this, but I believe it's our only hope.

If we are to survive, even thrive, in the days, weeks, months to come as a lesbian, gay, bi, trans, queer, pan, ace, intersex, or sexual or gender-expansive minority in this country, we will need to find solidarity with one another. We will need to get to know each other. You see, one of the great truths of humanity is that we are willing to defend what we love with our lives. Revolutionaries die for their friends, not the abstract principles they gather around.

Me, my partner, and the rest of the crew got Tuesday Mornings in Hillcrest, San Diego covered. It would be great if one of you gets Tuesdays somewhere else, and we would love to hear from you.

In the final analysis, we are the ones we have been waiting for; we are the ones who are going to turn all this awfulness around. Even if it's one cup of coffee at a time. One neighborhood at a time. One morning at a time. ▇

The author standing next to the Coffee and Class Solidarity sign (photo courtesy of the author).

lenny duncan (they/them) is a writer, scholar, lit agent, and cultural producer working at the intersections of Black liberation, spirituality, and art. The bestselling author of Dear Church, *they are also the author of* United States of Grace, Dear Revolutionaries, *and* Psalms of My People. *A PhD candidate at the Graduate Theological Union, lenny seeks bold, prophetic book proposals—works that fuse mysticism, rebellion, Black futures, queer theology, and radical imagination into transformative public scholarship.*

Celebrating

A professor in 1980s Brooklyn finds that surviving as Black overshadows surviving as queer. A polyamorous throuple in San Diego wins legal recognition as a three-parent family. An AIDS survivor pays tribute to those lost to the epidemic in 1980s San Francisco. These stories give us a host of reasons to celebrate, taking us to times that seemed to be the end but turned out to be a very strong beginning.

Selamlik and a Bouquet of Flowers on Jean Genet's Grave

By Khaled Alesmael

I **HAVE BEEN LIVING** in Morocco for some time now. I read; I write; I drink green tea, and every morning, I visit Jean Genet's grave. I turn my back to the prison wall and gaze at the ocean, reciting passages from *Selamlik* at his tomb. Then, I step into his house and jot down my thoughts in his garden. I will miss the peace of Morocco, far from the Levant's awakening.

"Genet wrote about Syria and Palestine!" says Naima, the cemetery caretaker, as she turns the key in the gate's lock, leading me towards the grave of Jean Genet (1910–1986).

I am in the city of Larache, Morocco, fulfilling a vow I made to myself years ago: To visit this graveyard and read an excerpt from my novel, *Selamlik*, in Jean Genet's presence. Some Western critics have drawn parallels between my writing and his, seeing in my work echoes of his cryptic explorations of love, homelands, and prisons. The most difficult kind of writing, I believe, lies in expressing the language of love for borders encompassing a place where you no longer belong.

It is January 1, 2025—a sunny day, warm as a summer afternoon in Northern Europe. I stand behind Naima who is wrapped in a thick wool dress, a wool hijab, and wool socks. She welcomes me and leads me into the cemetery.

A mother dog greets us with protective barking, her six puppies playing behind her. Holding a copy of one of my books, I follow Naima along a narrow, winding path lined with white graves of Spanish soldiers—a moving reminder of Spain's modern occupation of Northern Morocco.

Naima knows little about Genet beyond the fact that he wrote about the Middle East, spent his final years in Larache, "adopted" a young Moroccan man, and lived with him until his death. He requested to be buried on this hill overlooking the Atlantic Ocean.

Naima congratulates me on the fall of the dictator Assad and promises to open Genet's house for me after I finish my visit to the cemetery. Then she leaves me alone.

"Syria is free now and your grave guardian congratulates me," I whisper to Genet's grave—first in Arabic, then again in French: "La Syrie est libérée." I did not expect my visit to morph from a personal tribute into an overwhelming sense of victory—the triumph of revolution, the fall of Bashar al-Assad's regime.

In 2011, the dream of a free Syria was a collective vision that captivated most Syrians. It was perhaps a dream too vast for us to grasp, too heavy for us to bear. Non-violence wasn't just a choice; it was our only means to garner the world's empathy and send a message: "We did not ignite the fire; we were trying to extinguish it."

But what does "free Syria" mean today?

Standing at Jean Genet's grave, the Atlantic Ocean before me and the prison of Larache behind me, I grapple with questions: Does Assad's fall equate to Syria's freedom? Or is freedom something deeper than the absence of a tyrant? Is it the absence of fear? Or the ability to dream unshackled? From Genet's book, Prisoner of Love, I read:

"To fight for liberty is to want something undefined, something more than the end of oppression."

The term "New Syria," increasingly echoed in media and conversations, raises more questions than it answers. Are we truly witnessing a new Syria, or is it just a symbolic name for a political shift? This reminds me of "The White Protest" in Damascus—a demonstration largely comprised of LGBTQ+ Syrians in spring of 2012. This took place in a neighborhood where the community often gathered, a place mentioned in Selamlik: Sibki Park and Shalaan Avenue, streets lined with modern shops and restaurants. We chanted "Freedom!" raising our hands to the sky as though reaching for a vision of the future. But I remember how my friends were brutally arrested, their white shirts stained with blood. And another line from Genet's Prisoner of Love comes to mind: "Blood is always present in revolutions, but it is never enough to guarantee change."

Back then, demands included constitutional amendments, the abolition of unjust death penalties, and the granting of citizenship to children of Syrian mothers married to non-Syrians—at least to those with Palestinian fathers. There were calls to decriminalize homosexuality, with those condemned by Article 520 of the Syrian Penal Code by up to three years in prison.

Reality was unkind. The "Free Syria" we envisioned was a mirage, and every attempt to realize it was met with violence and repression. Now, with the regime's fall, have we moved closer to that dream?

The wall separating the Larache cemetery from the prison reminds me of the dichotomy that ruled our lives in Syria. Every moment of hope was countered by a moment of fear; every attempt at life, counterbalanced by an instance of death. Even here, I feel trapped between past and future, between the freedom we have always sought and the prison that still haunts our consciousness.

Jean Genet wrote about Syria, but the Syria he knew was under French colonial rule. That colonial legacy lingered, manifesting in Article 520, which criminalized same-sex relationships. Genet's Syria fought for freedom from an external colonizer. The Syria I carry within me fought for freedom from an internal oppressor.

As I left the cemetery with Naima, I recalled the Moroccans' prayers that Assad's fall would benefit Syria. Their words carried hope but also reminded me of the weight of responsibility. I wonder, can we, as a generation that lived through the revolution, build a New Syria? Can we redefine the concept of a homeland free from oppression and fear?

The New Syria isn't just a political state; it is a human, cultural, and social condition. It is an attempt to regenerate the Syrian soul, shattered over decades.

As I gaze at the Atlantic Ocean, I think of Syrians who crossed the waters to escape the war. How many Syrians now live across other seas, dreaming of a New Syria to which they might one day return, even if only on a fleeting visit? Migration was an unavoidable choice for many, yet it also marked the beginning of a redefinition of our identity. Syrians today are scattered across the globe, carrying their language and culture like their mothers carried vases of flowers.

Syria is not just a geographical entity but an emotional state, lived by Syrians everywhere.

I leave the cemetery, placing a bouquet of wildflowers and a copy of my novel, Selamlik, on Genet's grave. The mother dog is quiet now, nursing her puppies.

Naima invites me for a cup of Moroccan tea and a short rest at Genet's house, which is just one block away from the cemetery. The house is empty except for his library. I sit on the stairs next to his bookshelf, packed with French books about the Middle East, North Africa, and Islam, and write lines for this article.

As it turned out, my visit to Jean Genet's grave wasn't just to pay respects to a beloved writer and my inspiration. It was an opportunity for me as a proud Syrian to reflect on our past, present, and future.

A free Syria—or a New Syria—isn't just a slogan; it's a long journey requiring courage, patience, and faith. As we, a generation that lived through the revolution, carry this immense responsibility, we must write our own story, telling the world what it means to reclaim a homeland, to fall, to rise, and to keep dreaming.

Genet reminds us: "Words are weapons, but only if they reach the ears of the powerful."

I am gay, Syrian, a writer. It is my duty to write what I feel about my country. This is what Genet did and this is what readers remember. A battle has been won but there is more to do!

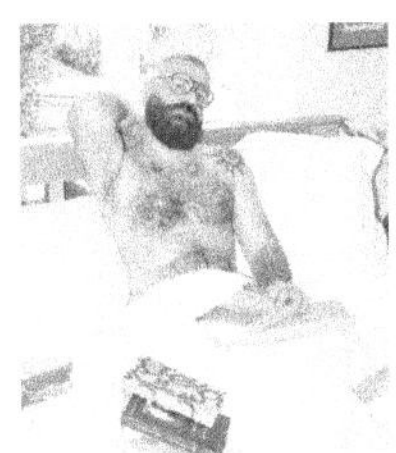

The author visiting Jean Genet's house in January 2025.
[Photo: Juan Gomez Delgado]

Khaled Alesmael is a Syrian novelist and short story writer based in London. He studied English Literature in Damascus University and has seen his literary works translated from Arabic into multiple languages worldwide. Khaled is the author of Selamlik *(2024) and* Gateway to the Sea *(2027).*

The Luxury of Being Gay

By Charlene Bryant

I GREW UP IN one of the worst neighborhoods in New York City. East New York, Brooklyn, didn't really give you a lot of opportunities to explore your sexuality. The East conditioned you to explore methods to stay safe, to stay alive.

Across Linden Boulevard were the worst projects in NYC, the Louis Pink Houses, and across the street was Howard Beach, Queens. Howard Beach was primarily an Italian-American neighborhood. John Gotti lived in Howard Beach. Those who lived there made sure to communicate the message that blacks were not allowed.

On December 20, 1986, a young black man from Crown Heights named Michael Griffith, was riding his bike in Howard Beach. He was murdered during an attack by a white mob as they chased him out of the neighborhood. Just like Willie Turks and Yusef Hawkins, Griffith was killed by the rampant racism that many people do not realize existed in New York City.

While walking home from a friend's house around that time, a blue Cadillac filled with white boys pulled up next to me and the guy sitting on the passenger side said, "Get out the neighborhood, nigga." I thought for sure I was going to get pulled into the car. Instead, they laughed and drove away.

I was mugged at nine years old and the clarinet loaned to me by the school for practice was stolen. The much older black kid that took it also punched me in my face: a parting gift. He was found dead a few weeks later.

Me and my homegirls watched where our friend Kathy's brother lay dead for hours. He was shot under my window, and the killers left his body for the neighborhood to discover.

It was normal to hear random gunshots popping off at night. The walk from the Grant Avenue train station to the building was like walking through a mine field. You knew you were safe when you saw the drug dealers at their stations.

Being black in America is a job; being gay is a luxury. Being gay could be turned off or hidden, but being black was like being a police officer: it always made me a target. Everybody in my neighborhood knew I was gay. But no one ever thought to comment about it. We were all too busy being black.

I came of age in the West Village. My academic, cultural, and sexual growth was enormous. I attended NYU and met different people and had many interesting experiences. But most importantly "the Vill" taught me that I was kind of not alone. It was a place where I could experience other people like me. I say "kind of," because I have been ostracized by my LGBT siblings for being black.

I was in Chelsea one day. Two friends and I were shopping along 8th Avenue when we walked into a nice-looking clothing store. Now two of the three of us were earning six-figure salaries. We were well-dressed and not looking like—whatever a thief looks like. That didn't stop the white shop boy from following us around the store. I really couldn't believe this was happening. When we confronted him with his racist tactics, my law degree served its purpose. After my verbal onslaught he finally blurted out that because we were black, we presented the possibility of theft.

That experience and a few others had me confused. The LGBT community was constantly advocating for equal treatment, equal rights—the same rights black people and other oppressed communities were struggling to obtain. I thought since we shared a common goal, we moved as a collective to obtain equal rights for all. I was wrong.

I never had to "come out." I've seen and heard so many stories about how people had to struggle to be themselves. Gay people struggling to be accepted. Why must anyone seek the acceptance of others about who and what they are—how God made them? I was very clear about who I was from a very early age. I didn't struggle with it; I was proud of me. Most importantly I never cared what other people thought of me. I still don't allow myself to be judged or defined. Before I am anything else, I am black in America. There are some of my gay "family" members who will not miss an opportunity to remind me of my blackness in the most derogatory way. Without reservation, gay people will treat me with the same violence they fight against. They fight for white gay acceptance, not black.

My parents and ancestors taught me many things. They taught me how to fight. My great-great-grandmother was a freed slave. My grandmother, a member of the Great Migration, worked as a cleaning lady at night. I have used every modality of violence and intellect to get here, to pay homage to my ancestors.

Today I am an assistant professor at LaGuardia Community College. I teach my students the importance of education. I talk to them about not allowing people to take away their power. I convince them to acknowledge they are not "minorities," and they come from cultured civilizations. I try to get them to accept that they can make a difference in this world where their membership in a protected class creates the illusion of disempowerment.

My students have shown me that today being "gay" is fluid. As I experienced many years ago, my students don't spend so much energy defining their sexuality. Many of my students don't feel compelled to justify their sexual orientation. I love it. They love who they want to love. They don't make excuses for what they are not. They see that hate and ignorance is endemic in this country, no matter who you love.

Charlene Bryant is a native New Yorker, college professor, and an avid sneakerhead.

On Writing
Black Queer Fiction

By Mecca Jamilah Sullivan

"So, your mother is a Black feminist? No wonder your writing is so queer!"

I gave a quiet chuckle over the rim of my drink and nodded. I was with a new friend at one of Washington DC's many chic Black bar restaurants. Stylish couples lined the walls, hair done, shoes on point, radiant in their summer best. All the couples, as far as I could tell, seemed straight. My friend and I, both Black, queer women, guessed that the host, the server, and the smiling manager who came to greet us were all family. Either way, the night was queer to me: "The Glow of Love" by Change featuring Luther Vandross blared across the dining room, and my friend and I bobbed our heads in shared reverence, reading queerness between the lines, delighting in Luther's voice, this unspoken icon of black, queer life and love, singing: *It's a pleasure when you treasure all that's new and true and gay...*

We were celebrating my novel, *Big Girl*, which had just been shortlisted for an award for LGBTQ fiction. I was excited. All writers like recognition, but this was especially meaningful for me. The novel is about a big, tender-hearted black girl who comes of age in 1990s Harlem, fighting against inherited legacies of body shaming and gender stigmas passed down over three generations of women in her family. The novel means a lot to me, partly because the story is similar to my own, and partly because of how much I learned from the character herself. Malaya, the novel's protagonist, is inquisitive, quiet, and funny; she has the kind of complex, sometimes contradictory, inner life that I long to see in Black characters. She loves color and food and '90s hip-hop. She works hard to love herself. And she's queer.

As a writer, my characters' queerness is always as central to their stories as their Blackness, their gender, or their size. For me, this is what it means to create full characters: they have multiple facets, live in multiple worlds, and it's the precise alchemy of such multiplicity that defines them. As curious as Malaya is about food, she's equally curious about women's bodies. Both represent forbidden desires she can't resist, and stigmas she doesn't understand. This matters to me. I was, and am, grateful for every single reader. And yet, when *Big Girl* came out, I was surprised to find that, in some reviews, queerness appeared as a footnote to a larger story of Black womanhood. These reviews said the novel was about a fat, black girl fighting to make space for herself in the world. It was about gender, race, class mobility, gentrification, hip-hop, and fatness (a topic that is still rarely talked about in literature). But queerness, in some reviews, was often framed as mere experimentation, and sometimes not mentioned at all.

Of course, I shouldn't have been surprised. As a student and scholar of Black queer feminist thought, I know the traps of intersectionality well. Audre Lorde, Cheryl Clarke, Pat Parker, June Jordan, and many others remind us how seductive—and how dangerous—it is to use one aspect of identity (like race or gender) to write queerness out of our life stories. As Lorde puts it, "there is no such thing as a single-issue struggle, because we do not live single-issue lives." When we fail to acknowledge this, the cost is not just personal, but political. When a story about a fat black queer teenage girl becomes a more general story about body positivity, for example, not only does the character flatten, but the social stakes of the story thin away.

I thought about this as Luther's chorus rolled full and thick through the low-lit restaurant, my new friend singing along. She had not yet read the novel, and when I told her about it, she asked how the story came to me. I said what I often do: that like my protagonist, I grew up as a fat, Black girl in Harlem, that I was constantly aware of what my body meant to people around me, and how everyone wanted my body to change in ways I could not fully grasp. It was Black feminist literature that helped me through the landscape of my body's meanings, I told her. I shared how reading Jamaica Kincaid, Toni Morrison, and Ntozake Shange as a fifth-grader helped me understand how Black girls' bodies are treated as property, as objects, and how such treatment is often the projection of oppressive fantasies of power. I told my friend how these books showed me where black girls' bodies fit into a historical nexus of race, sex, class, and gender—configurations in which Black women must fight to define and claim our humanity and create our freedom. I told her how, even at that young age, reading these stories helped me feel more powerful and less alone. Finally, I told her I discovered these books not at school, but in my mother's small Black feminist library in the basement of our home in Harlem.

Cover of Jamilah Sullivan's 2022 novel, *Big Girl*.

"So, your mother is a Black feminist?" She sipped her mezcal, the ice clinking against the glass as she raised her eyebrows in a smirk. "No wonder your writing is so queer!"

I lifted my own drink, a paloma, and smiled back. I hadn't thought about it that way, but it was true. While I was poring through my mother's library, pressing my chubby fingers over the slick first-edition cover of Kincaid's *Annie John*, sniffing the powdery paperback pages of Morrison's *The Bluest Eye*, and holding up the cover of Shange's *for colored girls who have considered suicide when the rainbow is enuf* in the mirror so that the thoughtful, yearning Black girl face on Shange's cover sat parallel to my own—I was discovering myself in Black feminist literature, and also recognizing myself in the queer parts.

In each of these books, race and womanhood are inseparable from delicious intimacies shared between Black girls, and I couldn't get enough. I read these books ravenously in the quiet of the basement, often whispering the juicy scenes to myself so no one would hear. I studied the moments in Annie John when Kincaid's young narrator discovers her freedom in illicit games of Black-girl pleasure held during recess at her repressive postcolonial Caribbean school. I admired the ardent, nearly-chivalrous devotion that drives Morrison's narrator, Claudia, to care for the outcast Pecola Breedlove when their community rejects her for being too dark-skinned in *The Bluest Eye*. I delighted in the sensual ways Shange's eponymous "colored girls" moved and healed and touched each other as they told their stories of sex, trauma, and love through *for colored girls who have considered suicide when the rainbow is enuf*. In each of these stories, I discovered that same-sex intimacy, desire, and love are what make freedom possible.

And yet, though many scholars have explored the queer resonances of these and other Black feminist works, none of these stories are widely understood as queer. There are many reasons for this. As writers publishing in the 1970s and 1980s, Morrison, Shange, and Kincaid had little incentive to claim any non-heterosexual identity for their characters, at least from a publishing standpoint. Some black women writers, like Morrison, have explicitly rejected readings of their characters as gay, while others, like Shange, have embraced queer themes and welcomed queer readings of their work. We need these writers' works regardless. We need their racial histories, their class and gender critiques, and their queerness, explicit or not.

But for me, it's important to say it clearly: My books are queer. I would no sooner quiet my characters' queerness than I would their blackness, or their womanhood. I know many contemporary queer writers feel this way. Writers like Marci Blackman, Nicole Dennis-Benn, Ana-Maurine Lara, Janet Mock, M. Shelly Connor, Darnell L. Moore, and many others draw on the legacies of Black feminist literature, naming our characters as LGBTQ+ and make explicit the "new and true and gay" that has lived at the center of our literary traditions forever.

We name our characters' queerness for ourselves, for our readers, and for the sake of the queer futures we hope our work makes possible—futures in which the many truths of Black, queer life can be spoken, written, and read out loud. I told my friend this, too. Then we laughed and kept singing.

Mecca Jamilah Sullivan, PhD, is the author of three books: Big Girl, *a* New York Times *Editors' Choice and winner of the Balcones Fiction Prize, and the Next Generation Indie Book Award for First Novel;* The Poetics of Difference: Queer Feminist Forms in the African Diaspora, *winner of the William Sanders Scarborough Prize from the MLA; and the short story collection,* Blue Talk & Love, *winner of the Judith A. Markowitz Award from Lambda Literary. She has earned honors from Bread Loaf, the Institute for Citizens and Scholars, the Mellon Foundation, the Center for Fiction, the NEA and others. Originally from Harlem in New York City, she is a professor of English at Georgetown University in Washington, D.C.*

Three Dads and a Baby

By Ian Jenkins

FEW PARENTS HAVE TO GO to court to win parental rights. Parentage is assumed for almost everyone—but if your kids are carried by a gestational surrogate, a judge has to grant you custody. The process usually goes so smoothly that the "intended parents" don't need to appear in court. But we did. We weren't asking the San Diego Superior Court to implement a standard, lawyer-approved surrogacy contract. We wanted our judge to grant at-birth custody to three fathers—me and my two partners, Alan and Jeremy—something that had never been done anywhere in the world.

In our minds, it was only natural for all three of us to have custody because our child wouldn't have existed without all three dads. Alan and I had wanted children, but we hadn't made the leap to creating any. We faced real hurdles since neither of us had a uterus. Then we met Jeremy. The three of us began dating, became a family, and combined our homes into one. Jeremy pushed us to imagine the joy kids would bring and to make parenting a reality.

Of course, the women in our lives made it all possible. Friends Julie and Stephanie offered us unused embryos from their IVF family efforts. Meghan offered to go through egg harvesting. Alan's good friend Delilah offered to carry our child because she wanted to see more love in the world.

Then a team of lawyers labored over all the contracts and family plans needed to move ahead with surrogacy. After all the legal hurdles, right before our planned implantation, our surrogacy doctor torpedoed all of our plans. She claimed to have concerns over managing our surrogate's risk of contracting Zika, a virus that can be spread to a fetus and cause birth defects risk. However, as a doctor myself, I'd read up on all the issues, and I knew she wasn't following professional guidelines. Something else was afoot, something that felt related to our being three dads—and we scrambled for another doctor as our scheduled implantation date rapidly approached.

Our new doctor, thankfully, supported us completely. He prepared Delilah for pregnancy, implanted our embryo, and managed some scary complications to get us to the third trimester. But despite all the hurdles, even assuming childbirth went well, we still faced a huge challenge: simply being allowed to be our child's parents.

We asked the court to make a polyamorous family the legal parents of a child for the first time. At first, the judge kindly explained that while she presided over Superior Court, hers was still a lower court, and she was in no position to set precedent. She had to follow existing law. And California law said extra parents could be added to a birth certificate only when not having the extra caregiver as a legal parent presented a serious detriment to the child.

It was a class "catch 22": we had to prove there was some "detriment" to our child, but no child existed as yet. How could our lawyers convince the judge to break with precedent and permit us to be parents when our child had yet to be created? The judge could not recognize an unborn child's parental needs.

My heart sank as I saw our plans slipping away. I worried that I would be some kind of weird housemate to our child's two legal parents, not an equal partner: I would have no formal parental rights. Our lawyers struggled to change the judge's mind, but she shook her head and sighed as they spoke. I knew it wasn't working.

Then Alan went full mama bear. He interrupted the court proceedings, poking our attorney, insisting on speaking. He addressed the judge when she noticed and asked her to swear us all in. Two minutes later, we'd taken our oaths and stood to address the court, asked for a legal first, and fought for our unborn daughter. There have been three parent families before—as when a lesbian couple added a sperm donor friend as a parent when the kid was old enough to understand, or when a dying mother retained parental rights while her child underwent adoption by a couple before she died. But no court anywhere had ever recognized a polyamorous family as the legal parents of a child at birth until that day. We became the first because my partner insisted. The judge couldn't deny us as our child's three dads once she heard how much we loved and wanted to share in raising our baby-to-be. Her pronouncement of our parentage felt like the joyous climax of a tense legal drama.

I'd never been so proud. I'd grown up thinking I'd never even be able to get married or even share a nice Christmas together with a partner and our families. Instead, we've managed to build a unique modern family through perseverance and an amazing team of friends, lawyers, doctors— and an obscene financial toll.

Judges all over the West Coast have heard our story, and unique loving family arrangements are now an option for others, too. For our second child, we didn't even have to go to court! We received his polyamorous-gay family birth certificate—the second ever—with no trouble or drama whatsoever.

Love makes a family, and love is what makes our family a wonderful home for our children. Love, our wonderful families, our accepting friends and community—and a little assistance from a California court.

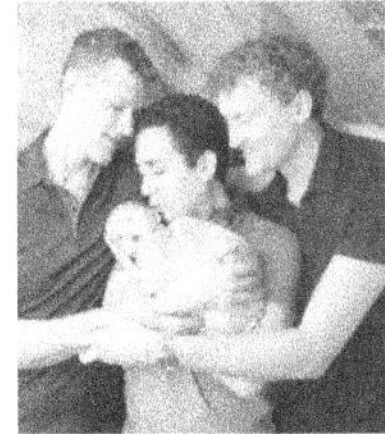

The author and his family.

Ian Jenkins and his two partners, Alan and Jeremy, became the first polyamorous family in history to be the legal parents of children on a birth certificate. They told their story in Three Dads and a Baby: Adventures in Parenting, *making the news on five continents and paving the way for other poly families. Their exceptional kids, Piper and Parker, suffer from an over-abundance of love.*

Bruce and James

By Héctor Vizoso

On halloween night in 1991, the doorbell rang, and it was Bruce. He was excited and hurried in to tell me to get ready because he had enrolled us in a Halloween competition at the After Dark in Monterey. I said I didn't have a costume, and suddenly, as if out of thin air, there appeared two large, colorful flowers. Bruce said, "I made them, and you just need to wear black, but hurry; it's almost time for the competition." When we got to Lighthouse Avenue, we parked and placed these enormous flowers on our heads. He gave me two branch petals, and we walked into the bar. Everyone turned to look and, for a moment, it was exhilarating. Soon the competition started, and we were third to go up onto the stage. At that moment they were playing Madonna's "Vogue," and Bruce and I started to vogue using our petals. The crowd applauded and laughed, and like a miracle, we danced on stage as if we had rehearsed these moves for several days. We were awarded second prize, but for several days thereafter I felt we had won first prize. I believe we received a check but can't remember the amount; I just remember that wondrous night at the After Dark.

Bruce was diagnosed with AIDS a few years prior, in 1989. His partner, Richard, would travel with him from Monterey to San Francisco to obtain care, and when he returned from these visits, he would tell me all the stories of his treatments, the people he met, and the new therapies he received. When he started taking AZT, we all felt hopeful, but that hope did not last long. Bruce did not respond well to the drug, but never once told me he was scared or angry. As his illness progressed, I wanted nothing more than to help him, but felt inadequate to do so. Bruce was hospitalized and released so many times in that period that I lost count.

During one of those visits, I arrived late to the hospital and heard a loud wailing. It was coming from Bruce's room, and I heard his partner, Richard, sobbing uncontrollably by Bruce's bedside. I hesitated to enter the room, feeling frightened. I realized at that moment I had lost my best friend. When I did enter, I saw Richard lying next to Bruce on the bed, holding him tightly and sobbing. All I could do was stand and wait. When Richard composed himself, he asked if I could drive him home because he was not able to drive. I said yes, and before I left the room, I looked at my friend, who was almost unrecognizable from when we first met. His life had just come to an abrupt end, and I was unprepared for the void it caused in my life. My friend was gone at age thirty. I gently kissed him on the forehead and took a deep breath, and walked out of the room holding back my tears. A few days later, I dreamt about Bruce and my dog Beau, who had also recently passed away. Bruce appeared in my dream, and I asked, "What are you doing here?" He said, "I have a surprise to show you," and then Beau appeared. He was wagging his tail. Then Bruce waved, and they both walked away, causing me to wake up. Bruce was happy, shining brightly as always, and he stopped to tell me that Beau was all right. Bruce was the first of many friends that would pass away quickly. Each time, the void I felt became bigger and bigger. And then, almost six months later, Bruce's partner passed away driving home one night from work; he was killed by a drunk driver. I think Bruce missed Richard very much and wanted to be with him for eternity.

A few months after Bruce passed, I received a call from my cousin James, who was living in Miami. He told me he had been diagnosed with HIV. He cried, and I asked him what I could do. He was silent, and immediately I told him he had to come to Monterey to visit. When he finally came shortly after, I picked him up at the airport, and he looked like he had lost a lot of weight. Never did he talk about HIV or AIDS, until one night in San Francisco after taking mushrooms and dancing all night; we came back to our hotel room, and he told me that when he dies, he wanted me to call his parents and send his mother a Mother's Day card, which I told him I would. I asked him if he regretted anything. He replied, "Nothing." James and I had had so many crazy escapades in our lives, and our time together was always filled with adventure, sometimes chaos. We talked about our childhood until the sun came up, the friends we had known and lost, and life in general. Little did I know this would be the last time I would physically spend time with James. Soon after he was hospitalized multiple times, and each hospitalization became a long-distance telephone call. He felt isolated, and for the first time ever, I felt he was lonely. Although his family and friends visited, he knew that time was not in his favor. I did eventually fly to New York to visit him in the hospital. He had a tumor in his brain, and was undergoing radiation only to keep him comfortable. James' light had vanished. The spontaneity and the joy were gone. Soon after my visit, he was moved to hospice, and he passed away a month later. I did not attend the funeral. I just could not say goodbye. Like with Bruce, James' death left a black hole in my life that would take many years to fill. And I lived with survival guilt. I had done everything James' and Bruce had done, but I was not sick. It took some therapy to resolve this guilt, and I still think about them both. They still live within me, but I can't pick up the telephone to talk to them except in my mind. Every now and then something will happen, and I will say to myself: if only James and Bruce could have seen this.

Every now and then, I am reminded of many old memories with them, and I start to sob. I don't know why, except the light seems to flicker much more now that I am 62. I have so much to be grateful for, but the darkness surrounds me so intensely that I can't find my way out. I keep looking for Bruce's beacon and James' light. I know I need to create my own light, but it would be so much easier if they were still around to take me on one of their adventures. ▪

Héctor (left) and Bruce at After Dark in 1991.

Héctor Vizoso is a retired nursing director and AIDS researcher whose essays blend personal reflection with historical insight. His work, published in peer-reviewed nursing and medical journals, explores the enduring impact of the AIDS epidemic and the human stories within it. His essay "Night Shift," published in the American Journal of Nursing *(2022), received an APEX Award in 2023.*

My Daddy's Daughter

By Noni Salma

I.

THIS IS NOT A LOVE STORY. Or a story of a child missing a father. This is a story of a father chasing a lost shadow. This is a story of a child who is not a dream come true.

II.

There are different names you can call your male parent. One is Father. Another is Daddy. Depending on your relationship with him, one might fit like a glove while the other feels like a horse swapped midstream.

I call mine Daddy because that's what we always called him. He was the man who, during my childhood, hovered like candle wax mid-drip, ready to burn at the grazing of skin; the one I grew up learning like a map.

Da-dd-y. Although we've been estranged since 2016, it would be wrong to call him anything else because the image stuck in my head is who he was to me; the man who raised me.

III.

I have another father who I call Papa.

Papa has an infectious signature smile that causes everyone to smile back. Sometimes when I'm cooking, Papa walks into the kitchen for something, like a glass of water or a toothpick, and when our eyes meet, he breaks character because we both know that he's spying on the cooking, hoping to have a bite and talk. He does a little dance while the hot, slippery fried plantain wiggles around his tongue. Papa's presence is an ingredient in whatever food I am making. Especially the Jollof rice; his facial expressions toward each pinch of spice or ounce of water serve as a map guiding me.

Unlike Daddy, Papa doesn't pray to a sky god. But he says "amen" whenever someone prays for him. He tells me that the reason he does this is because he believes in spiritual energy, and whatever someone believes to be true, is their truth.

Papa loves to share a glass of bourbon with me every Friday while he listens to me rant about schoolwork, the challenges with my writing, or some boy issues. Papa likes to listen to the boy stories because I struggle to talk to him about them. It is important to him that I feel like I can be vulnerable with him. Papa wouldn't use words like "should," but would nod to everything. He has a slow nod that indicates he's not in support of something, like when I told him I wanted to tattoo my boyfriend's name on my ass crack.

He has another nod to indicate he was still following the story I was telling him and was acknowledging when I arrived at a new beat.

My favorite nod is the one he does to signal he agrees with my point of view. I could be talking about how blaming only the Nigerian leaders for the country's shortcomings wasn't enough and that everyone needed to change from top to bottom because the rot was already within. He would pause and give me a knowing look, the one he gives whenever he wants to buttress a point of mine. And it would end in us downing our glasses, as if in celebration of our father-daughter synergy.

I watched him play Nat King Cole's "Unforgettable" on the stereo. When the music hit a crescendo, he transformed into a one-man show. His body is made for dancing. He moves purposely, but with swagger, and he accelerates at every beat of the music. Papa dances as if dancing for a packed audience. He dances with confidence, even when no one is watching. Even when my back is turned against him, I can tell when his fingers are doing a snap or when his feet are doing the tap. I can tell when he's humming silently to himself, and I can tell when he's performing the words of the song with his burly body.

His body told stories of its own the way his smile usually did. His unbridled energy called out for mine to come home with him. We'd share his dance floor. No matter how hard I tried, I never was able to match his vigor and stagecraft, but it didn't deter me from trying. And he'd flash me a smile whenever I made a signature move, as if to tell me that he loved it, as if to tell me to just have fun and that it wasn't a competition. He'd remind me why the song remains an all-time favorite.

When I eventually underwent sex reassignment surgery in January 2018 in New York City, Papa was there; he flew all the way from Nigeria to be a hand-grab away from me. And when the anesthesia wore off and I was conscious enough to recognize him, he leaned over and whispered to me, "hey daughter."

IV.

I imagine Daddy has his own version of me, a child he had instead of me. A boy called Bubba.

You would think Daddy coughed him out because of how similar they both are. Bubba would be one of the young leading Muslim brothers at the Ansarudeen mosque, where Daddy was the chairman of the division. Unbeknownst to all, Bubba would have a drinking problem he hides from everyone, because he has to be a perfect son.

Even in my own imagination of who I think Daddy wants me to be, I fail. He already has a flaw. Bubba drinks and gambles. Bubba prays five times a day and mutters "salaam alaikum" to every room he enters, even if it's his own room that only he inhabits. Bubba always ends every sentence with, "by god's grace." But Bubba's eyes always wander and undress all the women at asalat. Even the ones old enough to be his mother.
Still, Bubba is Daddy's perfect son.

V.

What do you call a male parent who is no longer in your life? I don't mean dead. Because that would mean you're fatherless. Is there a word for a father who decides you are persona-non-grata? Ex-father, maybe? The way your boyfriend becomes your ex-boyfriend. See why I call him Daddy? That seems like a word that is immovable. Daddy is not a title. It's an event that happened.

VI.

I was in a Manhattan restaurant in July 2016 for a friend's birthday dinner when my friend W. asked if I heard that my family had disowned me. He said it the way you inform someone that their favorite restaurant closed down. Disappointing, but not tragic.

Before that moment, I started medical and social transition, and did an interview with an online radio I thought nobody listened to. I had jokingly even said to a friend that it probably would be listened to by five people, and I would be one of them. But that interview found its way out of the obscure network into the page of a popular Nigerian journalist, which snowballed into a viral media sensation in Nigeria. Like everyone else, Daddy found out about his daughter through the worldwide web.

My body did her thing by first being calm. Then it sprung up in jitters, like a cold shower on a limp body. It wasn't as if I didn't see this coming. It wasn't the first time Daddy toyed with the idea of disowning me. All the days of my incessant running away and Grandma advising him to, and the days I heard him wondering if he made the right choice by not listening to her.

It had finally happened. My father, breaking up with me.

I went to the bathroom for a pee break with the hope of getting the tears out. Nothing. It was the reflection of me in the mirror that made my eyes cloud with coated tears. My simplistic, burgundy jumpsuit with bohemian beaded necklace and slick-back hair made for quite the view.

Looking back at me: the becoming. A flight mid-air, ready for take-off. I was the miracle that almost didn't happen. And it broke my heart that somebody could choose to want no part of it.

I was living in New York, but was making headlines in Nigeria, because even in 2016 for Nigerians, being a trans woman was akin to being a cannibal. The headlines were brutal.

Whoever the person they plastered across the headlines was, I didn't recognize her. I must have got lost, somewhere between the misgendering and deadnaming, between the curses in the comment sections and the pearl-and-purse-clutching.

There is a kind of death that happens when you see your image decimated in the press, when people decide who you are and tell it to themselves and other people.

It's a nameless death, and I'm still yet to find my body.

Noni Salma is a Manhattan Film Festival, Queer West African Women's Writing Contest, and GLAAD List Award-winning screenwriter, actress, and filmmaker whose eclectic works are largely inspired by her experiences growing up in the colorful city of Lagos, Nigeria.

A Journey to Self-Acceptance

By Chenoa Rai

"**Can i have a purse?**" I asked Big Mama. I was five years old.

After asking me why I wanted it, my big mama purchased me one. I wore my purse with confidence and pride—in the house. I was never instructed to wear it only in the house, but I sensed that it was our little secret and I kept it as such.

Over the next few months, I pranced around putting anything and everything into my purse, just as I'd seen my mom and big mama do. It was my introduction to womanhood, and it brought me such joy. My joy would come to an end whenever I heard the rattling of house keys, which meant my dad had arrived to pick me up.

And back to reality I went. I would put back on my masculine mask and enter the world of boyhood as if nothing ever happened. I did this for years, wearing my mom's clothes and shoes, wrapping a towel around my head to give me the illusion of long flowy hair, and imagining myself as the woman I was born to be. Pretending behind closed doors was the only time I was allowed to truly be myself, because in the "boyhood" world of sports, I did everything I could to fit into the box I was supposedly born into. But whispers began to linger in the air, and "sissy" and "soft" were terms that began to be associated with me.

Knowing what my teammates, parents, and family thought of me, I worked on perfecting my craft as a basketball and baseball player, so I could be known for being more than a sissy. Athleticism was my way of deflecting and changing my image. When that didn't work, humor became my armor. But humor could only suppress my emotions for only so long. On the inside, I was crying out to live my truth, but the world did not allow this.

A Black boy feeling like a woman and wanting to live as one: where was this acceptable? Definitely not in my world, and I didn't have the language to properly express who I was. The only trans representation I had came from Jerry Springer, who did more to exploit trans women than to humanize them.

It wasn't until I read Janet Mock's article "I was Born a Boy" that I finally felt I had a place. Reading writer, director, and advocate Janet Mock discuss her upbringing, her sense of being born in the wrong body, her struggle for self-acceptance, the challenges she faced, and the steps she took to live in her truth, I knew I'd found my counterpart. I'd found a woman whose story paralleled my onw. I, too, dreamed of being a journalist living in the city, writing pieces that moved people. Janet Mock breathed life into me as a trans woman who lived a normal life, a powerful counterweight to the depiction of the ladies on Jerry Springer as "freaks" and "female impersonators." I immediately began learning more about Janet Mock's story, and in doing so I came across Isis King, Carmen Carrera, and Candis Cayne—all women like me.

Seeing them allowed me to envision myself as I've always wanted to be: a woman living the American dream. But this vision became blurry when reality sank in. How was I going to tell my homophobic family that I was transgender? Although my family wasn't visibly homophobic, they definitely made jokes that made me uncomfortable. Plus, I didn't think they'd comprehend the difference between gender and sexuality. It's a debate that much of the world has yet to grasp.

Still, the more research I did, the more I felt I belonged. I went into a deep dive listening to interviews of my trans sisters telling their stories of heartache and acceptance. I smiled with joy knowing that one day I too would feel this whole as myself. With that joy came pain, though. The murder rate for Black transgender women began to skyrocket, pushing me back into hiding out of fear for my safety.

I already have to deal with being Black in America and the risk that comes with that, but the vulnerability of being Black and trans is even greater. Facing all of this discrimination and hatred, I became depressed and questioned if living my truth was worth possibly losing my life.

Thankfully, I spoke to a therapist who helped me win my battle against depression and accept myself for who I am, for better or worse. I took my first hormone replacement shot on August 14, 2016 and never looked back.

While things were looking up, I still hadn't informed my family, both because I didn't feel the need and because straight and cisgender people never have to come out as such, so why should I? I was in no rush to have that conversation with my parents. But eventually I decided to tell them I was trans. For a year, I would set a date to come out, the date would come and go, and I'd rinse and repeat.

Finally, in the spring of 2017, I wrote a letter to my big mama where I expressed my love and told her I was transgender. As I placed the letter on her nightstand, my heart pounded with negative thoughts and the fear that this would be the end to our relationship.

Later that night, Big Mama called. "I already knew. I was just waiting for you to accept yourself. And know that nothing would stop me from loving you." As I cried on the phone, I felt a weight lifted off my shoulders. I felt free.

It took me sixteen years to accept that I was a woman, and while it took my parents longer than Big Mama to accept me, they eventually did so. I came out just in time to walk across the stage as an out trans college graduate, and as I did, I knew I was walking into my destiny as my truest self.

Chenoa Rai (she/her) is a freelance journalist from San Francisco, California. A proud transgender woman, she loves live-tweeting, watching salacious reality shows, and attending and viewing comedy shows. Most of all she loves getting lost in romance novels.

Acknowledgments

LET ME AGAIN THANK Allison Armijo, whose pivotal role in the "Here's My Story" story is discussed in my general introduction. Allison joined us in early 2023, but HMS has a pre-history going back to 2019, during which time the column was edited in-house and posted sporadically. Among those who made an early contribution were Art Cohen, Sam Dapanas, and Paul Fallon.

From the start, HMS has been managed and overseen by *G&LR* publisher Stephen Hemrick, who brought together the needed resources, worked with the Boston Web Group on technical matters, and often did a final edit before posting a story.

This book would not be possible without their efforts, not to mention those who worked on this project. For the design and layout of the book, including the cover, we have artist Rick Fiala to thank. We're grateful to Sam Dapanas for proofreading, fact checking, and editorial assistance. And special thanks to *G&LR* contributing artist Charles Hefling for his helpful critique.

I'd also like to thank the Board of Directors of *The G&LR* for their ongoing encouragement and support for this project. And a very special thanks goes to the Leonard-Litz Foundation for underwriting an important part of this project.

Finally, our warmest gratitude goes to the many hundreds of individuals who have shared their stories with us over the years, and especially to those who consented to publish their stories for a new readership in this book.

Richard Schneider Jr.
Editor-in-Chief, The G&LR